# The Basics of
# Rubber Stamping

believe dream

aspire to BE

dream

believe

aspire to BE

DREAMS ARE THE TOUCHSTONES OF OUR CHARACTERS

# Table of Contents

**S**tamping in its most basic form is applying an inked rubber image to a given surface and coloring it. That's all! But, it's also so much more. And once you understand some of the possible techniques, there is no limit!

**I**n this book, we'll show the tips, tools and techniques that will allow you to take your stamping to a new creative level. We'll start with the basics—explaining what tools and supplies are available. Then we'll look at some of the techniques and the results you'll achieve with them. We'll also look at the various surfaces you can stamp.

**A**nd that's where the fun begins! Here are dozens of creative stamping projects—from cards and gifts to jewelry and home décor. They've been designed to inspire your creativity and give you the ideas and the know how to make your own stamped masterpieces. They're projects you can be proud of yet, in the end, they all come down to the basic idea of an image applied to a surface with color.

**Y**ou're invited you to explore new techniques, discover new stamping supplies, find your own style and let your creative side soar! (We'll hold your hand and give you tips along the way.) Enjoy!

3

## Types of Stamps

The essence of stamping is to create beautiful images—and there are thousands of stamps for you to create your own beautiful projects. Several basic factors are involved when selecting stamps: the size of your project, the surfaces upon which you'll be stamping and how precise you want your stamping compostions. Here are the basic types of stamps:

### Wood-Mounted Stamps:

These are the first choice of most stampers and usually offer the highest quality. The rubber stamp surface is mounted onto a wood block, with the image inked on the back for easy recognition. The wood block offers a good surface to hold for cleaner, more precise stamping. They come in a wide variety of sizes, shapes and designs.

### Foam-Mounted Stamps:

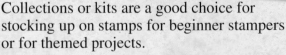

These stamps most often are sold in collections or kits and are usually less expensive than wood-mounted stamps. The rubber stamp surface is mounted directly onto a foam backing. Collections or kits are a good choice for stocking up on stamps for beginner stampers or for themed projects.

### Acrylic-Mounted Stamps:

These stamps are mounted on a clear, acrylic block. The transparent mounting allows you to see exactly where your stamp image will be applied. Acrylic-mounted stamps are great for aligning multiple images.

Ink is almost as necessary to rubber stamping as the stamps themselves. There are many types of ink available: some for specific effects, some which adhere to certain surfaces and others which are more appropriate for archival projects. Note: Store your ink pads upside down so the pad stays moist.

**Dye-based inks:** These inks are fast drying and tend to hold fine detail very well. They adhere to most surfaces—from glossy to matte. Some are acid-free and perfect for archival projects, especially scrapbook pages. Many are water-based and work well with blending techniques to create a watercolor effect. Others are washable and great for crafting with children.

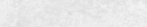

**Pigment-based inks:** These inks are slow drying, opaque and lend themselves well to embossing. Most pigment inks dry only when heat set. Many are archival and permanent. They come in a wide range of colors, including metallic sheens and Petalpoint™ ink pad collections.

**Chalk inks:** These inks are relatively new and combine the quick-drying time of dye-based inks with the rich color content of pigment inks. They can be embossed on glossy surfaces and are permanent when heat set. They dry to a muted, chalk-like finish.

**Acrylics:** Many home décor paints are acrylic based. They dry quickly, adhere to most surfaces and come in a myriad of colors. Acrylic paints come in liquid or spray forms.

**Sealer & Varnish:** A sealer prepares wood, papier mâché, ceramics and other porous surfaces for stamping or painting. It also works well on glass. Varnish is a protective finish applied to a surface after all stamping and embellishing.

# Cutting & Folding Tools

**X-acto® knife:** This craft knife is invaluable for cutting out windows and for fine detail. Use a sharp blade and a cutting surface, such as a self-healing mat to protect your work space.

**Metal ruler:** A metal ruler provides exact measurements, a straight edge for cutting and folding; or an edge for tearing paper against.

**Bone folder:** This device can be used for scoring and folding; or for burnishing metal (see page 9).

**Scissors:** A good pair of sharp scissors is a must. There are also pattern-edge scissors available for fun edges.

**Paintbrushes:** There are a variety of styles and sizes available, but there are a few musts for stamping. ← The *stipple brush* is a stiff, bushy brush used for speckling ink or paint (see page 7). A thin *flat paintbrush* can be used to fill in empty spaces, while the wider ones are used for painting larger areas. A *foam brush* is perfect → for applying sealer or varnish because it doesn't leave bristle marks. It is also inexpensive and cleans up easily.

**Sponges:** There are two types of sponges recommended for stamping. *Foam sponges* absorb ink and paint nicely. They are ideal for edging or blending and come in square or triangle shapes. *Sea sponges* come in irregular shapes and textures. They are great for applying inks or paints for colored accents.

**Chalks:** Decorative blending chalks are great for adding subtle color highlights to paper and vellum surfaces. They provide a watercolor effect and blend well with other colors for a variety of hues. Use your finger, a small foam applicator or a cotton swab to apply the chalk. Decorative chalks usually come in multiple packs of squares. (Don't use sidewalk chalks as they won't adhere well to paper.)

# Adhesives

There are many adhesives available. Most are formulated for specific purposes.

**Glue stick:**  The glue stick is easily available and works well with paper.

**Tacky craft glue:**  This basic glue works well with paper, fabric, plastic and wood.

**Glue Dots™, Mini Glue Dots® & Pop-Up Glue Dots™:** These are great for quick and easy assembling. They give dimension to the material behind which it is placed.

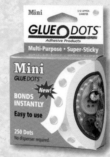

**Foam adhesive tape:** This double-back tape comes in strips, squares or sheets and provides dimension. Use two layers for extra depth.

**Terrifically Tacky Tape™:** This double-back tape is ideal for adhering micro beads or other tiny lumpy embellishments.

**Low temperature glue gun:** The glue gun is ideal for crafters for adhering unique embellishments.

**Decoupage glue:** This product works as an adhesive for paper collage techniques.

← **E6000® or the Ultimate glues:** These are industrial strength glues. They're ideal for adhering items to glass and ceramics.

# Embossing Tools

**Embossing powders:** When this powder is applied to pigment ink and heated, it melts into a glaze that leaves a raised image on your project. It's available in transparent, opaque, metallic and glitter finishes.

**Embossing heat tool:** This high-powered blow dryer generates a stream of hot air to melt wax and plastic. It's used to dry ink onto paper, thereby making it permanent. When used with embossing powder and ink, it heats the two substances into a glaze.

# Embellishments

**Eyelets:** Eyelets (or grommets) are those little round metal circles that attach layers of paper or other thin materials in place for a decorative, yet functional effect. They come in a variety of colors.

**From left:** Handheld → hole punch, hammer, anywhere hole punch and eyelet setter. (The anywhere hole punch is shown below.)

**1** From the front of the paper, punch a hole with the anywhere hole punch. Then insert the eyelet.

*step 1*

**2** From the back of the paper, use the hammer and setter to pound down the edge to secure the eyelet.

*step 2*

# One-Color Stamping

To apply ink to the stamp, lightly tap (don't rub) the stamp onto the ink pad for even coverage on the raised areas of the stamp. It's important not to rub the stamp on the pad as it will cause the ink to build up unevenly on parts of the stamp. Foam pads tend to need lighter pressure, whereas felt pads work well if you use more pressure on the stamp.

## Multi-Color Stamping

Using the same inking guidelines as one-color stamping, you can use more than one color to create a gradient or multi-color effect. Ink one end of the stamp with one color, then continue with different colors to cover the stamp image. This technique is great for creating a rainbow effect. Using small ink pads are best for this effect as they are easier to handle in a small area. Also try dipping a sponge onto the ink pad, then pressing it onto the stamp to ink specific areas on the stamp.

## Sponging Techniques

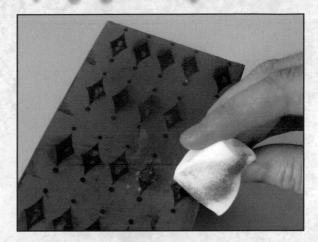

Dab your foam sponge into the ink pad until it has taken on the color of the ink, then lightly dab it onto your project for a subtle effect or smear it on for a blended look. The more ink you apply, the darker and more dramatic the effect. You can obtain a multi-color effect by sponging several colors onto your project.

## Stippling

Use a stipple brush to apply ink onto a surface for creating a softer effect than that of sponging. This technique is ideal for creating an aged look along borders. Simply tap the bristles onto the ink pad, hold the brush straight then gently tap the brush up and down onto the surface.

# Collage Techniques

**Collage stamps:** Some rubber stamps feature ready-made collage-style images and are most convenient for a collage look.

**Collage with multiple stamps:** There's no limit to the number of stamps or styles to create a collage composition. You can develop a theme of coordinating images or try completely different ones. Add some non-stamp embellishments (beads, skeleton leaves, charms, fibers) for a wonderfully unique look. Remember, there's no limit!

**Decoupage collage:** Though similar to collage, decoupage emphasizes overlapping images and objects. Step 1: You can either stamp on paper, then tear around the images or randomly tear pieces of paper, then stamp on them. Step 2: apply decoupage gel to the back of each paper piece as you place it on your surface, then continue by overlapping additional paper pieces to cover your surface.

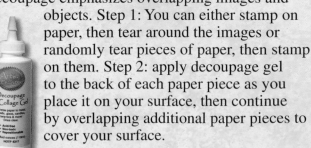

# Random Stamping

Repeating stamped images on a surface creates a unique background. It's best to choose an ink color lighter than the one you'll use for the main focus image. Re-ink the stamp and change the angle of the image for the random effect.

# Continuous Stamping

This technique is ideal for covering large areas. You can align the stamped images for a uniform look or slightly change the alignment for a different effect. Use a ruler as a guide to make a uniform look.

# Direct-to-Paper Inking

For the direct-to-paper technique, remove the ink pad cover. Place the ink pad directly onto the surface you wish to cover. Either tap it for lighter ink coverage or smear it for a thicker, complete coverage. With smaller paper pieces, place scrap paper behind them to protect your work surface.

**Heat setting:** Applying the embossing heat tool over stamped or sponged areas will make the ink permanent. Most heat tools are designed to be held 6"–8" above the surface and should be moved back and forth to prevent overheating on one area. For special heating, such as preparing wax, it's best to practice on an old candle.

**D**istressing techniques give your project an antique look and work on just about any surface. When the ink is still wet, wipe the image with a dry paintbrush or smear it with a foam sponge for an aged effect. Once the ink is dry, lightly sand or scrape random areas to accent those pieces.

**Embossing with ink & powder:** Stamp the image onto your surface. While the ink is still wet, sprinkle embossing powder on top. Place the embossing heat tool over the image and move it back and forth until the powder turns into a glaze-like finish.

## Masking

**M**asking is a way to protect a previously stamped image when creating a 3-D effect by overlapping images. To begin, stamp a clean image on what will become your finished project. Next, stamp the same image on a scrap piece of paper. Once the ink has dried, cut out the scrap paper image as closely as possible. Place the second image on top of the first, then stamp other images around it without affecting the original stamped image. Remove the scrap piece and you'll discover a delightful effect!

**Embossing Metal:** This technique, also known as *burnishing*, involves pressing a bone folder or stylus onto thin metal to create grooves or valleys. It works ideally with large design stamps. To create an embossed metal image: Ink your stamp and press it onto the metal surface. Place the metal onto a soft foam surface (such as a computer mouse pad) or a kitchen towel and trace over the stamped image with the bone folder or stylus. When you turn the metal piece over, the effect is a raised embossed area.

*stylus*

*bone folder*

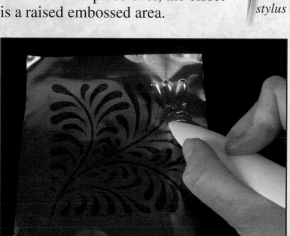

# Paper

**Glossy paper:** It's non-porous finish is perfect for stamping and holding all types of inks, though heat setting is recommended when using pigment inks. There are acid-free varieties of paper and ink available to use in scrapbooking or other archival projects.

**Matte paper:** This non-shiny paper is ideal for stamping as it provides a clean surface for the ink with little risk of smearing. It holds any type of ink well, though heat setting makes the ink permanent.

 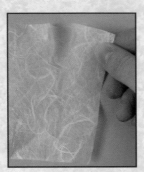

**Handmade paper:** There is a myriad of textures and grains available. Mulberry paper (shown here) is one of the most popular and lends itself well to stamping and collage. To tear the edges, wet the area which you wish to tear and pull it gently upward for a feathery edge.

# Papier Mâché

The texture of papier mâché is slightly smooth, though it tends to curve irregularly. You may have to roll the stamp along the surface to get a full image. You can stamp directly on papier mâché or cover it with paint, fabric, paper or other elements. To stamp directly onto papier mâché, apply a sealer to the surface so the ink has a better surface on which to adhere.

# Vellum

Vellum's transluscent quality adds visual depth to your stamping project. Due to its non-porous surface, dye-based and chalk inks work best because they dry quicker. With any ink, it's recommended to heat set the ink to make it permanent. You can stamp on a single layer of vellum, or place vellum over your stamped image for a ghosted effect. Vellum is ideal for insertion into windows or frames.

# Wood

Many wood surfaces can be stamped, but you'll probably want to test how your ink reacts with the wood before stamping the whole piece. If you're unsure, apply an acrylic sealer onto the wood surface. The sealer provides an ink-friendly surface on which to stamp. Chalk inks are best for wood, but pigment inks work fine if heat set. To protect the completed wood project, apply a coat of acrylic varnish over the entire surface.

The smooth surface of glass and ceramics can make stamping challenging, but the result is worth it! It's best to practice on a sample piece to get the feel for stamping on smooth surface. There are inks formulated just for glass or ceramics, but others can be used if you seal the surface first with an acrylic liquid sealer and heat set the ink. Terra cotta is so porous that it must be sealed prior to stamping. This procedure should only be used for decorative pieces. When working with a curved surface, place the inked stamp on the surface and roll it to stamp the entire image.

## Candles

You can stamp directly on wax or on paper and glue it to the candle. The result of direct stamping is an antique effect. If you want more vivid color, once the wax has cooled and the ink has dried from direct stamping, use a small tip paintbrush to add more ink or paint to the stamped image. Vellum's transparent quality provides a perfect background for stamped images on wax.

## Polymer Clay

Stamping on polymer clay (Fimo™, Sculpey®, etc.) results in a recessed image in the clay. Start by rolling out the clay, stamping the inked image into the clay then follow the manufacturer's instructions to bake the clay. Pigment inks work best with polymer clay.

Fabrics with a smooth finish and tight weave work best for stamping and embossing. Cotton, silk, muslin and leather are all good choices. Stamps with bold images work best, as more detailed stamps loose their clarity on fabric. While crafting inks or fabric paints work best on most fabrics, permanent inks work better on leather. It's important to seal leather with a leather sealant after stamping to protect the completed project. Our designers chose Fiebing's Leather Stampables Sheen (a liquid acrylic sealant) though there are other sealants available at most craft or fabric stores.

Time for heat setting fabric will vary (20–60 seconds) depending on the iron, heat setting and contents of the fabric. You may wish to practice on a scrap piece of the fabric you wish to use in your project to determine the best combination of heat and time.

## Velvet

Velvet is ideal for embossing! When a stamp is placed on the nap (fuzzy) side of the velvet and heat from an iron applied to the fabric, the velvet compresses and keeps the impression of the stamp. Bold images work best with this technique. To heat set, preheat the iron to wool or cotton setting with no steam. Place the stamp face up on an ironing board, spray the nap side with a mist of water, then place the nap side face down over the stamp and hold the iron steady over the velvet for 10–30 seconds. Remove the iron and let the velvet cool before removing the stamp.

# Plastic

**N**ow there's a great use for that unwanted CD! First, sand off any finish from each side, then apply a liquid acrylic all-purpose sealer to the side on which you'll stamp. The sealer prevents the ink from bleeding. After you've stamped your image, heat set the ink, then reheat the plastic slightly to make it easier to cut.

# Shrink Plastic

**S**tamp your image on shrink plastic with dye-based or chalk ink. Use strong, sharp scissors to cut out the image, then follow the manufacturer's instructions to bake the plastic. Remember to punch any holes before baking. The image will shrink to ⅓ of the stamped size!

# Metal

**T**o prepare a metal surface for stamping, wipe it with white vinegar or lemon juice to remove any residue. Pigment inks should be heat set onto metal and dye-based inks should be sealed with varnish to protect them from flaking.

# Sealing Wax

**C**reate great medallions by stamping into a melted pool of sealing wax. Sealing wax comes in a set of disks or a stick that are easy to use. Place a disk on a sheet of waxpaper, use an embossing heat tool to melt the wax, then place an inked stamp gently into the wax and allow the wax to harden before removing the stamp. When the wax has cooled, carefully lift it from the wax paper and glue it onto your project.

# Craft Foam

**T**his thin craft foam holds ink very well. Dye-based inks work best with craft foam so you don't have to heat set it. You can stamp anything onto craft foam as you would paper surfaces. Craft foam can be found next to the felt in most craft stores.

# A Stamping Secret!

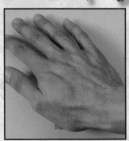 

**F**or perfectly stamped images every time, place the inked stamp on your surface and apply light pressure onto the stamp with the palm of your hand. To finish, hold the stamp with one hand and use your thumb to press along the edges.

Your rubber stamps are an investment that should last for years. With that, caring for your stamps is important, but shouldn't be difficult. One thing to keep in mind is never immerse your stamps in water. There are many liquid cleaners or wipe cloths available to make the job quick and easy. Use an old toothbrush to clean ink from any crevices. Allow the stamps to dry thoroughly before storing them. Store your stamps image side down and out of the sunlight. You'll find these easy steps will keep your rubber stamps looking new for a long time.

## Bows

### Puffy Bow:

**1** Beginning with one end of the ribbon, wrap it around your thumb to make a center loop.

**2** Make a loop on one side of your thumb, give the ribbon a twist, then make another loop. Continue making loops at the same length until your desired number is reached.

**3** Bring the ribbon end up and hold it at the back of the bow, then cut it in the bottom center to form two tails. Insert a length of wire through the center bow loop and twist the ends together to secure the bow.

### Shoestring Bow:

**1** Measure the desired tail length from one end, then make a loop and wrap the free end loosely around the center.

**2** Form a loop in the free end, push it through the center and pull the loops in opposite directions to tighten.

## Jump Rings

To open a jump ring, separate one end to the left and the other end to the right with flat nose pliers. (Don't pull the ends apart as it will distort the shape.)

To connect two jump rings, separate the ends of one ring, slide the other ring onto the opening of the first ring.

To close the open jump ring, use flat nose pliers to push the two ends together.

## Scoring

Place a metal ruler on the paper along the line you wish to score, then run the back edge of an X-acto® knife along the ruler edge to form a crease. Fold the crease inward.

## Tracing & Transferring

Trace the pattern with a pencil onto tracing paper (or, if using vellum, trace the pattern directly onto the vellum sheet). Cut along the straight outer lines. Dashed lines represent areas for folding or when designated, the halfway point to turn the vellum over and trace the other half of the pattern. Be sure to erase any stray lines.

## Threading a Tag

Fold the fiber in half. Thread the fold through the hole from the back. Thread the fiber ends through the fold. Pull the ends to remove the slack.

# Paper

Paper is the most popular of rubber stamping surfaces. It's so versatile and there are so many varieties—from traditional glossy and matte, to exciting new handmade papers and vellums. Here are 10 projects for you to discover your own creative style.

# Decoupage Tray

rubber stamps:
  Stella's Gone to the Bank (dress form)
  My Mother's Dress
  Minnie
  Leaf Whimsey
  Lettre
  Believe
Enchantment Petalpoint™ Ink
Royal Blue pigment ink
purple embossing powder
medium blue acrylic paint

12"x8¼" unfinished wood tray with cut-
  out handles
white cardstock
3"x6" tag
dark purple embroidery floss
metallic multi-color embroidery floss
gold charms:
  two 1¼" single leaves
  one ¾" two-leaf twig
  one 1¼" three-leaf twig
  one ⅞" sunface

4" length of 1½" wide gold metal mesh
  ribbon
six gold 3mm E-beads
decoupage glue
liquid acrylic all-purpose sealer
liquid clear gloss varnish
tacky craft glue
1" wide foam brush
fine grain sandpaper
embossing heat tool

**1** Seal the tray (see page 5) and let dry. Paint the tray with two coats of blue paint; letting each dry thoroughly between coats.

**2** Stamp and tear the following cardstock pieces: Lettre with blue ink on a 3½"x4"; Believe with blue ink on 5"x1½"; Minnie with purple ink on 2"x4½"; Leaf Whimsey with blue ink on 3"x4, 5"x3", 2¼"x3" and 1"x2½" pieces. Stamp Lettre in blue ink on the tag. Heat set each piece (see page 9). Stamp Stella's Gone to the Bank in purple ink on a 1½"x5" cardstock and My Mother's Dress on a 4½"x3½" cardstock, then sprinkle purple embossing powder on top of the wet ink on each and heat set. Cut around the dress image. Sponge (see page 7) the edges with blue ink on Minnie, sprinkle embossing powder on top and heat set.

**3** Tear a 1½"x5½" cardstock piece in a slightly triangular shape. Sponge various colors onto each stamped cardstock piece and heat set. Brush purple ink along the edge of the Believe and smallest Leaf Whimsey piece, sprinkle purple embossing powder on top of the wet ink and heat set.

**4** Wrap the mesh ribbon around the tag bottom, wrapping the ends to the back and glue to secure. String the beads onto the center of a 16" length of floss, fold it in half and thread it through the tag hole, knotting the floss ends together. Apply a thin layer of decoupage glue to the tray inside, then layer the pieces onto the tray as shown, with the tag and beaded floss centered at the bottom and the Believe centered in the middle of the tray. Apply decoupage glue to the collaged section, press the charms onto the paper pieces as shown. Apply a thick coat of decoupage glue onto the entire surface and let dry.

**5** Wrap floss around each handled and apply decoupage glue on top to secure it in place; let dry. Apply varnish to the entire tray and let dry. Repeat with another coat of varnish and let dry.

15

# Southwest Terra Cotta Pot

rubber stamps:
  Gecko
  Pottery
Espresso chalk ink
white mulberry paper
4½"x4" terra cotta pot

liquid acrylic all-purpose
  sealer
decoupage glue
1" wide foam brush
embossing heat tool

**1** Apply sealer (see page 5) to the inside and outside of the pot; let dry.

**2** Tear the mulberry paper (see page 10) into 3" squares. Stamp each piece with *Gecko* or *Pottery* with ink and heat set (see page 9).

**3** Place one stamped mulberry piece on the pot and apply decoupage glue to secure it. Overlap another piece onto the pot and repeat until the entire outside and top rim is covered. Apply an even coat of decoupage glue and let dry. Apply a coat of sealer to the entire surface and let dry.

## For other uses:

This pot is designed for decorative use only. If moisture seeps into terra cotta any stamping, painting and attached embellishments will be destroyed. To protect the pot for other uses, place a plastic liner inside. Plastic liners are available at most garden stores.

# Decoupage Butterfly Vase

rubber stamps:
  Butterflies Collection
  Fern
chalk inks:
  Brushed Sage
  Evergreen
  Lavender Flower
  Pink Porcelain
white mulberry
  paper
2¾"x5½" clear
  glass vase
decoupage glue
1" wide foam brush
embossing heat tool

**1** Stamp an assortment of *Butterflies* onto the mulberry paper (see page 10) with the blue, lavender and pink inks, allowing ½" space between the imprints. Use the sage and evergreen inks to stamp the *Fern* onto the mulberry paper, also leaving ½" space between each imprint. Heat set (see page 9) the imprints then tear each out, leaving ½" of paper around each image.

**2** Apply decoupage glue to the back of a stamped piece and place it on the vase. Repeat to cover the entire vase with a fern centered around butterflies, overlapping the mulberry paper edges and wrapping the top pieces to the vase inside.

**3** Apply a thin coat of decoupage glue over the entire vase surface and let dry.

# Heirloom Quilt Box

rubber stamps:
   Heirloom Quilt
   Made With Love By
chalk inks:
   Painted Desert
   Espresso
copper pigment ink
clear embossing ink
embossing powders:
   clear
   copper
light ivory acrylic paint
5"x8" cream suede paper
4"x6" white mulberry
   paper
ivory cardstock
5"x3¼"x3⅛" unfinished
   wood box
3½"x2½" piece of
   polyester fiberfill
metallic gold cord
5" of natural twine

buttons:
   four ³/₁₆" wide dark red
   one ³/₄" wide burgundy
   one 6mm red pony
      bead
⅛" wide silver
   eyelet
eyelet setting tools
pattern-edge scissors:
   pinking
   deckle
1" wide foam brush
sewing needle with
   large eye
liquid acrylic all-
   purpose sealer
Pop-Up Glue Dots™
paper towels
red pen
fine grain sandpaper
low temperature glue
   gun, glue sticks
embossing heat tool

**1** Apply a coat of sealer (see page 5) to the box and let dry. Lightly sand the box and wipe clean. Paint the box ivory, then use paper towels to wipe off the excess paint to reveal the wood grain; let dry. Apply a coat of sealer and let dry.

**2** Stamp *Heirloom Quilt* on suede paper (see page 10) with brown and red inks and heat set (see page 9). Stack the stamped paper onto another piece of suede paper and cut around the image with the pinking scissors, leaving an ⅛" along the long sides and ½" on the short ends.

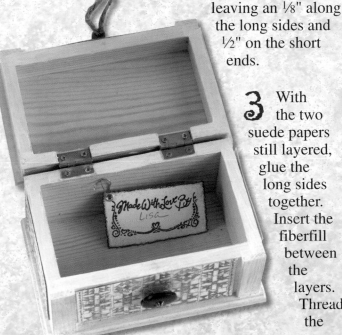

**3** With the two suede papers still layered, glue the long sides together. Insert the fiberfill between the layers. Thread the needle with gold cord and sew each end together, knotting the ends on top. Glue a small button to each corner. Tear a 5"x3¼" rectangle of mulberry paper then glue it to the box top. Glue the stamped quilt centered on top of the mulberry paper.

**4** Cut two 2⅜"x1¾" and one 3½"x1¾" rectangles of ivory cardstock. Stamp *Heirloom Quilt* onto each piece with a mixture of inks and heat set. Cover each piece with embossing ink, sprinkle clear embossing powder on top of the wet ink and heat set. Glue a smaller piece to each box side and the larger one centered on the box front.

**5** Fold the twine in half, thread the bead onto the ends then knot the ends together. Cut off the tails close to the knot. Glue the knot to the lid center front. Layer two Pop-Up Glue Dots™ together on the box center front to attach the large button, threaded with gold cord, so the twine loop fits easily around the button.

**6** Stamp *Made With Love By* onto ivory cardstock with copper ink. While the ink is still wet, sprinkle copper embossing powder on top and heat set. Trim the edges with the deckle scissors. Brush the edges with copper ink, sprinkle copper embossing powder on top and heat set. Insert the eyelet into the upper left corner and thread a 2" length of gold cord through the eyelet. Write your name on the card and insert it inside the box.

# Renaissance Mosaic Bookmark

*Renaissance Mosaic rubber stamp*
*chalk inks:*
 *Spanish Sand*
 *Espresso*
 *Painted Desert*
*gold metallic pigment ink*
*gold embossing powder*
*cardstock:*
 *2⅛"x5¼" white*
 *2⅜"x5½" burgundy*
*liquid clear gloss varnish*
*10" length of burgundy embroidery floss*
*four ³⁄₁₆" wide gold eyelets, eyelet setting tools*
*½" wide foam brush*
*stipple brush*
*foam sponge*
*4 paper clips*
*embossing heat tool*

**1** Stamp *Renaissance Mosaic* onto the white cardstock (see page 10) with red ink. Randomly sponge (see page 8) tan and brown inks onto the cardstock; heat set (see page 9).

**2** Stipple (see page 7) gold ink onto the cardstock at the top, bottom and lower left corner. Sprinkle gold embossing powder on top of the wet ink and heat set. Use the foam brush to apply a coat of varnish over the cardstock and let dry.

**3** Center the stamped cardstock on top of the burgundy cardstock and secure with paper clips at the top, bottom and sides. Attach an eyelet (see page 6) in each corner to permanently secure the pieces together, then remove the paper clips.

**4** Fold the floss in half, thread the loop through the upper left eyelet and pull the ends through the loop to secure. Knot the floss lengths together 2" from the tail ends.

# Doggy Gift Box

rubber stamps:
  Dog & Hydrant (set of 2)
  Kitty Cat Paw Border
chalk inks:
  Espresso
  Painted Desert
gold metallic pigment ink
gold embossing powder
brown wrapping paper
gift box
2½"x4" corrugated cardboard
2½"x4" burgundy cardstock
3¼"x2" white paper
metallic gold embroidery floss
two 3/16" gold eyelets, eyelet setting tools
1⅓ yards of 1½" wide gold iridescent
  mesh ribbon with wire edges
black pen
22-gauge wire
wire cutters
X-acto® knife, cutting surface
clear adhesive tape
tracing paper, transfer paper
embossing heat tool

**1** Randomly stamp *Dog* and *Hydrant* (see page 8) onto the brown paper with brown and red inks; heat set (see page 9). Randomly stamp *Kitty Cat Paw Border* around the *Dog* and *Hydrant* stamps with gold ink. Sprinkle gold embossing powder onto the wet ink and heat set.

**2** Wrap the gift box with the stamped paper, using tape to secure.

**3** Trace and transfer the bone pattern (see page 13) onto corrugated paper and cut it out. Use the knife to cut out the center window. Cut a 2"x⅝" piece of white paper and glue it centered on the back of the bone. Mat the bone onto burgundy paper, leaving a ⅛" border. Attach an eyelet (see page 6) into each end of the bone. Use the pen to write a name on the white window of the bone.

**4** Cut four lengths of gold floss (length depends of gift box size). Lay them together, ends even, then place the box upside down onto the center of the strings. Wrap the strings onto the bottom, twist them once and wrap them to the top, turning the box rightside up again. Double knot the strings at the top so the ends hang freely. Cut four 18" lengths of gold floss. Hold them together and thread them through the top eyelet on the dog bone, pulling the ends even. Tie the ends to the string knot on the box top so the ends hang freely.

**5** With the ribbon, make a puffy bow with six 3" loops, one 5" and one 4" tail, leaving 1" lengths of the wire securing the bow. Trim each tail at angle. Secure the bow to the box top string knot with the wire tails.

19

# True Friend Window Card

rubber stamps:
  A True Friend
  Friendship Background
chalk inks:
  Pink Porcelain
  Blue Shadow
  Blue Suede
  Lavender Flower
  Pacific Horizon
two 5⅛"x7" glossy blank cards
16" of ½" wide dark teal satin ribbon
  with sheer edges
foam sponges
bone folder
Pop-Up Glue Dots™ & Glue Dots™
glue stick
X-acto® knife, cutting surface
embossing heat tool

**1** Stamp *Friendship Background* repeatedly to cover the card front (see pages 5 & 8) with Blue Shadow ink and heat set (see page 9). Lightly sponge (see page 7) Blue Suede, pink and lavender inks onto the card front and heat set.

**2** Open the stamped card face up on a cutting surface. Draw a 2½"x3¼" rectangle centered on the card front, then use the knife to cut an "X" inside the rectangle from opposite corners. Use the bone folder to create an crease between the corners on the top, sides and bottom to form a rectangle, without folding the sections back.

**3** Open the card. Sponge Blue Suede ink onto the inside front and heat set. Close the card and fold each section outward to reveal the blue side. Place a Pop-Up Glue Dot™ behind each section to secure it to the *Friendship Background*.

**4** Cut the second card in half along the fold and set one half aside. With the remaining half, sponge pink and lavender inks onto one glossy side and heat set. Apply glue along the left, right and bottom edges of the sponged side then glue it to the inside front of the first card so the sponged side shows through the card front window.

**5** Stamp *A True Friend* with various chalk inks onto the window panel so it is slightly offset and heat set.

**6** Use the ribbon to make a shoestring bow (see page 13) with 1½" loops and 5" tails. Trim each tail at an angle then use a Glue Dot™ to attach it to the upper left corner of the card front.

# Film Frame Photo Book

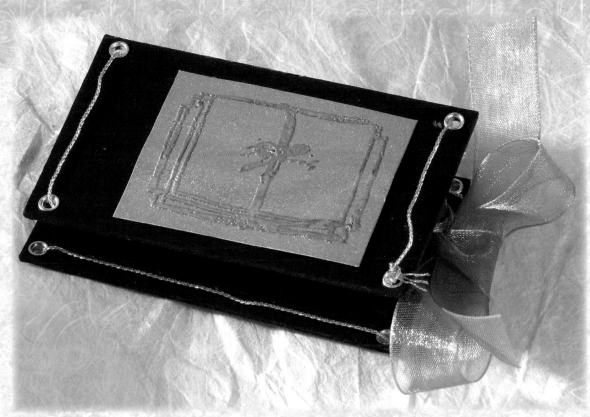

rubber stamps:
  Film Frame
  Love Letters
silver pigment ink
silver embossing
  powder
black matboard
Paper Pizazz® Metallic
  Silver paper
black paper
twelve 1¼"x1"
  photographs
16" of ⅝" wide silver
  sheer ribbon
metallic silver
  embroidery floss
eight ³⁄₁₆" silver eyelets,
  eyelet setting tools
clear adhesive tape
X-acto® knife, cutting
  surface
glue stick
embossing heat tool

**1** Stamp *Film Frame* six times (see page 5) onto black paper with silver ink. Sprinkle silver embossing powder onto the wet ink and heat set (see page 9). Place one stamped frame onto a cutting surface and use the knife to cut out the black paper around the frames to 2⅝"x1⅝". Cut out the window of each film frame, slightly smaller than the frame itself, leaving a ⅛" border.

**2** Tape a photo behind each frame window, then tape the six frames end-to-end to create a filmstrip. Cut six 2⅝"x1⅝" rectangles of black paper and glue one to the back of each frame piece.

**3** Cut two 3¼"x2" rectangles of black matboard. Attach an eyelet (see page 6) into each corner of each matboard rectangle.

**4** Cut the ribbon in half. Glue one end of one length to the back ends of the filmstrip. Glue the back of the right end section of the filmstrip centered on a matting rectangle, so the ribbon extends outward. Repeat for the left end section on the remaining matting rectangle. Fold the filmstrip into an accordian to close it, so the front cover is on top.

**5** Stamp *Love Letters* onto silver paper with silver ink. Sprinkle silver embossing powder on top of the wet ink and heat set. Cut the stamped image out to a 2⅛"x1⅝" rectangle and glue it centered on the accordian book front cover. Thread silver floss through the eyelets so it runs vertically on the front side and horizontally on the inside and knot the ends. Trim the tails close to the knots. Tie the ribbon into a bow to secure the book.

# The Arts Window Card

| rubber stamps: | 2"x4" black paper |
| Maintain Summer | white cardstock rectangles: |
| The Arts Collage | 15"x5¾" |
| Arch Perspective | 5⅛"x5¾" |
| Lettre | 4"x1½" |
| chalk inks: | two 3"x4½" rectangles of |
| Spanish Sand | ivory cardstock |
| Painted Desert | white acrylic paint |
| Lavender Flower | wire mesh |
| pigment inks: | two ³/₁₆" gold eyelets |
| metallic copper | eyelet setting tools |
| black dye | 12" of natural twine |
| decorative chalks: | foam sponge |
| yellow | decoupage glue |
| red | glue stick |
| purple | X-acto® knife, |
| blue | cutting surface |
| copper embossing powder | embossing heat tool |

**1** Place the large cardstock piece with the long sides on the top and bottom. Vertically score (see page 13) it 5" from the left edge, then again 4⅞" from the first scored line to form a Z-fold card (see diagram below).

**2** Sponge tan ink (see page 7) onto the entire card surface. Randomly sponge red ink (see page 8) onto the surface, then place wire mesh on top and randomly stamp more red onto the surface for a textured effect and heat set (see page 9). Place the wire mesh onto the surface and randomly sponge metallic copper ink onto the card. Sprinkle copper embossing powder on top of the wet ink and heat set. Stamp *Lettre* in various patterns onto the card with black ink and heat set.

**3** Place the card stamped side down, then fold the right end onto the back so the first stamped section is face up. Place the card on a cutting surface and use the knife to cut out a 2¼"x3⅝" window on the stamped section 1¾" from the right side fold and centered between the top and bottom edge, cutting through the two card sections. Cut four ¼"x2¼" and four ¼"x3⅝" strips of black paper. Open the card and glue the strips to frame the back of each window.

**4** Stamp *The Arts Collage* onto one ivory cardstock piece and *Arch Perspective* onto the other with black ink and let dry. Randomly chalk each stamped image with various colors. Glue *The Arts Collage* centered on the back of the card first section window and the *Arch Perspective* centered on the second window so each appears through the stamped window side.

**5** Refold the first section onto the second so the windows are aligned then add a dot of glue to each corner. Attach an eyelet (see page 6) centered above and below the front section window to secure the layers together. Cut two 6" lengths of twine and thread one through each eyelet, around the card edge and knot to secure.

**6** Stamp *Maintain Summer* onto the 4"x1½" white cardstock with lavender ink and heat set, then tear 3⅞"x1" around the stamped image. Use your finger to apply white paint to the ends to create texture and let dry. Use decoupage glue to attach the strip to the card inside back. Glue the remaining white cardstock rectangle to the card back to balance the card weight.

← *stamped side*

*card inside* →

22

# Birthday Scrapbook Page

rubber stamps:
  Dot Alphabet Collection
  Happy Birthday Collection
Pacific Horizon chalk ink
ivory paper:
  12" square
  5¼"x12"
3¼"x¾" strip of white paper
Paper Pizazz® blue vellum
1½"x2⅛" scallop-top white tags
  (total depends on letters in
  name)
1⅛ yards of ¼" wide blue satin
  picot ribbon
buttons:
  two ¾" wide blue
  two 1" wide ivory
  one ⅞" wide ivory
3/16" wide gold eyelets
eyelet setting tools
tacky craft glue
paper crimper
foam sponge
photographs:
  one 3¾"x5¼"
  two 1⅞"x1⅝"
black pen
embossing heat tool

1  Randomly stamp (see page 8) the *stars, birthday cakes* and *confetti* from *Happy Birthday Collection* onto the ivory paper square with blue ink; heat set (see page 9).

2  Crimp the 5¼"x12" ivory paper with the crimper. Place it on the stamped square, 1½" from the left edge. Attach an eyelet (see page 6) in each corner to secure it to the page.

3  Cut a 4⅛"x6¾" vellum rectangle. Randomly sponge it with blue ink; let dry. Glue the large photo to the vellum, ¼" below the top edge. Glue the small photos onto the crimped ivory below the vellum piece. Glue the buttons to the page as shown.

4  Place a 13" length of ribbon 2" from the right side of the page, then a 3" length around each right corner, gluing the ends at the back. Use an 8" length of ribbon to make a shoestring bow (see page 13) with ¾" loops and 1" tails, then glue it to the long ribbon, 1½" below the top edge.

5  Stamp a blue letter onto each tag, then sponge the edges and heat set. Place the tags in a column along the blue ribbon then attach an eyelet into each tag to secure them to the page.

6  Journal on the white paper with the black pen. Place it at a slight angle near the lower right corner of the page then attach an eyelet at each end to secure it to the page. Use the remaining ribbon to make a shoestring bow with ¾" loops and 2" tails, then glue it to the upper left corner of the large photo.

# Tags

dream

believe

aspire to BE

DREAMS
ARE THE
TOUCHSTONES
OF OUR
CHARACTERS.
·THOREAU·

The matte finish on most paper tags is ideal for stamping and embossing. The smooth, fairly non-porous surface holds all types of inks. They're so much fun to make, you'll find new ways to stamp tags for everything—from gift tags and cards to bookmarks and inspirational fans!

# Tri-Fold Sun Card

rubber stamps:
  Large Sun
  Celestial Collection
  Celebrate New
    Beginnings
  Ancient Text
chalk inks:
  Painted Desert
  Espresso
  Spanish Sand
two 2⅝"x5¼" ivory tags
¼"x¾" thin copper metal
6"x10" brown textured
  paper
12"x10" ivory cardstock

2½ yards of metallic gold
  cord
24" lengths of fibers:
  brown
  ivory
  lavender
two 24" lengths of
  natural raffia
stipple brush
⅛" hole punch
glue stick
X-acto® knife, cutting
  surface
metal ruler
embossing heat tool

**1** Stamp *Large Sun* onto a 4" square of cardstock (see page 10) with brown ink and heat set (see page 9). Cut around the sun rays of the stamped image. Stipple (see page 7) various inks along the edge. Glue the *Large Sun* to the brown textured paper, then tear it into a 3½" wide circle around the stamped image and set aside.

**2** Stamp *Ancient Text* in random patterns with brown and tan inks to cover each tag. Stamp *Sundial, Sun* and *Lunar Eclipse* from the *Celestial Collection* randomly onto each tag with various inks and heat set. Stipple various inks onto each tag and heat set.

**3** Cut the gold cord into 24" lengths and set two aside. Hold the remaining cords, raffia and fiber lengths together, thread them through one tag, pulling the ends even. Gather the lengths together next to the tag hole, wrap the foil strip around the lengths and pinch the foil ends tightly to secure the lengths together.

**4** Cut a 6" square of textured paper. Glue the tags centered side-by-side onto the textured square, with the fibers on the right. Glue the matted *Large Sun* centered between the two tags. Use the metal ruler as a guide and cut the piece in half down the center. Set the pieces aside.

**5** Cut a 12"x6" rectangle of cardstock. Score (see page 13) 3" along each short side then fold each side onto the front to form front flaps; then unfold the flaps and fold them to the back to keep the sides clear for stamping. Stamp *Celebrate New Beginnings*

onto the inside center with red ink and heat set. Stamp *Ancient Text* repeatedly around the *Celebrate New Beginnings* image, then randomly stamp images from the *Celestial Collection* in various inks surrounding the center image. Stipple various inks onto the entire center section and heat set.

**6** Punch holes an ⅛" apart along the top edge of the card inside. Insert two 24" lengths of gold cord through the left-most hole and lace it through the hole, wrapping it around the top edge and into the next hole until it reaches the right-most hole, knotting the ends at the card back and gluing them in place.

**7** Fold the side flaps onto the card front, then glue the *Large Sun* half onto each flap, aligning the edges.

inside the card

# Gift Tag Invitation

rubber stamps:
  Invitation
  Square Leaf Acrylic
chalk inks:
  Spanish Sand
  Espresso
$6\frac{1}{2}$"x$6\frac{1}{4}$" Paper Pizazz® ivory vellum
$3\frac{1}{8}$"x$6\frac{1}{4}$" ivory tag
$1\frac{15}{16}$"x$2\frac{11}{16}$" Post-It™ Note
scrap paper
two $\frac{3}{16}$" gold eyelets, eyelet setting tools
two $\frac{3}{4}$" gold double-leaf charms
20" length of $\frac{1}{2}$" wide gold sheer ribbon
16" length of metallic gold cord
24-gauge gold wire
foam sponge
stipple brush
wire cutters
embossing heat tool

*place on fold*

**1** Place the tag in the center of the vellum and wrap each side onto the tag front. Remove the tag and unfold the vellum. Lightly trace the triangle pattern onto the right vellum side, then turn the vellum over to trace the pattern onto the left side and cut out the corner to form a point on each front panel.

**2** Place the scrap paper inside the vellum wrapper and fold the front panels on top. Stamp *Square Leaf Acrylic* onto each side with tan ink and heat set (see page 9). Unfold the vellum wrapper and attach an eyelet (see page 6) into the front point of each front panel.

**3** Stamp *Invitation* onto the tag center with brown ink and heat set. Mask the scroll on the stamped image with the Post-It™ note. Sponge and stipple (see page 7) the chalk inks around the mask. Remove the mask and heat set. Cut an 8" length of ribbon and two 8" lengths of gold cord. Hold the lengths together, fold in half and thread through the hole, then thread the ends through the folded loop (see page 13). Trim the ribbon tails to 3" at an angle.

**4** Insert the tag inside the vellum wrapper. Insert the remaining ribbon through the eyelets on the vellum wrapper, pulling the ends even, then make a loopy bow with three 1"-$1\frac{1}{2}$" loops, one $1\frac{1}{2}$" tail and one 2" tail, securing the bow with a 12" length of wire. Coil each wire end around the eyelet setter and attach a charm at the end. Trim each ribbon tail at an angle.

26

# Framed Swirl Tag Card

rubber stamps:
  Dreams
  Framed Swirl
chalk inks:
  Pink Porcelain
  Spanish Sand
  Brushed Sage
gold metallic pigment ink
gold embossing powder
3⅛"x6¼" ivory tag
5"x7" blank glossy card
sage green paper:
  5"x7" rectangle
  2⅜" square
white paper:
  5"x5⅝" rectangle
  2⅛" square
  2½"x4" rectangle
two ³⁄₁₆" gold eyelets, eyelet setting tools
metallic embossed glass beads:
  one 8mm green
  one 6mm amber
brown fiber
natural twine
stipple brush
foam sponge
foam adhesive tape
glue stick
embossing heat tool

1 Glue the 5"x7" green paper to the card front. Stipple gold ink (see page 7) onto the card front and heat set (see page 9).

2 Stamp *Framed Swirl* repeatedly (see page 8) onto the 5"x5⅝" white paper to cover it with gold and green inks; heat set. Stamp *Framed Swirl* four more times on the square, overlapping the first layer with gold and green inks; heat set. Tear a triangle piece from the upper left corner to center of the right side. Place it on the card front gluing the left edge and attach an eyelet (see page 6) at each bottom corner to form a pocket.

3 Randomly sponge pink and tan onto the tag. Stipple gold ink onto the tag, sponge gold ink along the edges and heat set the tag. Cut 12" lengths of twine and fiber. Thread each length through the tag hole pulling the ends even. Thread a bead onto each twine end, then double knot the end to secure the bead onto the twine. Insert the tag into the pocket as shown.

4 Stamp *Framed Swirl* in the center of the 2⅛" white paper square with gold and green inks and heat set. Glue the stamped square centered on the green paper square. Turn the square on point. Attach it to the tag as shown with foam tape.

5 Stamp *Dreams* onto the remaining white paper with green ink and heat set. Tear around the stamped image. Sponge the torn edges with gold ink, sprinkle gold embossing powder onto the wet ink and heat set. Glue the piece to the card front pocket as shown.

# Inspirational Tag Fan

*rubber stamps:*
  *Folded Leaf Medallion*
  *Framed Swirl*
  *Baroque Vine*
  *Aspire to BE*
  *Dream*
  *Believe*
*chalk inks:*
  *Pink Porcelain*
  *Spanish Sand*
*metallic copper pigment ink*
*copper embossing powder*
*decorative chalks:*
  *purple, blue*
*tags:*
  *three 2½"x5¼"*
  *one 2⅛"x4¼"*
  *one 1⅛"x3¼"*
*beads:*
  *one 8mm copper embossed*
    *clear glass*
  *two 3mm clear glass*
  *one 8mm amber tube*
  *one 8mm metallic black tube*
*metallic embroidery floss:*
  *rose*
  *black with colored specks*
  *gold*
  *copper*
  *silver*
*liquid acrylic all-purpose*
  *sealer*
*chalk applicators*
*deckle pattern-edge scissors*
*foam sponge*
*tacky craft glue*
*tissue or soft cloth*
*embossing heat tool*

**1** Use the chalk applicators to blend various colors onto each large tag and the small tag. Use a tissue to rub off the excess chalk. Lightly spray each tag with sealer (see page 5) and let dry.

**2** Stamp *Dream* onto the center of the small tag with copper ink. Sprinkle copper embossing powder on top of the wet ink and heat set (see page 9). Stamp the outer edge of *Framed Swirl* four times onto the tag surrounding *Dream* with tan and heat set.

**3** For the first large tag: Stamp *Aspire to BE* as shown with copper ink. Sprinkle copper embossing powder onto the wet ink and heat set. Stamp *Baroque Vine* in random patterns (see page 8) onto the tag with tan ink and heat set.

**4** For the second large tag: Stamp *Baroque Vine, Framed Swirl* and *Folded Leaf Medallion* onto the tag in random patterns with copper ink. Sprinkle embossing powder on top of each image while the ink is still wet and heat set.

**5** For the third large tag: Stamp *Believe* as shown with copper ink. Sprinkle copper embossing powder onto the wet ink and heat set. Stamp *Folded Leaf Medallion* and *Framed Swirl* in random patterns onto the tag with pink ink and heat set.

**6** Trim each tag edge with the deckle scissors then sponge the edge (see page 7) with copper ink. Sprinkle embossing powder onto the wet ink and heat set.

**7** For the medium tag: Use the direct to paper technique on the entire tag with copper ink, then sprinkle copper embossing powder on top and heat set. Repeat the process two more times for a thick layer. Ink the *Framed Swirl* stamp with copper ink. Sponge the entire tag once more with copper ink, sprinkle embossing powder on top and heat set. While the layer is still hot, press the pre-inked stamp diagonally onto the tag and allow to cool. Gently remove the stamp and let dry completely.

**8** Cut the following floss into 20" lengths: 4 copper, 4, gold, 3 black, 3 silver and 2 rose. Hold the lengths together, thread them through all the tag holes, layered as shown, and knot them next to the hole. Wrap a 12" gold floss length around all the strands 1" from the knot and use tacky glue to secure it. Thread the beads onto single lengths and knot the ends to secure.

28

# Magnetic Photo Frame Tag

Carved Flower rubber stamp
chalk inks:
  Pacific Horizon
  Brushed Sage
three 3¹⁄₈"x6¹⁄₄" white tags
metallic gold embroidery floss
eight ³⁄₁₆" wide silver eyelets
eyelet setting tools
two 8mm amber glass tube beads
two ¾" wide circle magnets

wave pattern-edge scissors
fine grain sandpaper
stipple brush
foam sponge
X-acto® knife, cutting surface
glue stick
pencil
clear adhesive tape
3" square photo
embossing heat tool

**1** Randomly stipple (see page 7) one tag with blue ink. Sponge the edges with blue ink and heat set (see page 9).

**2** Randomly stipple the second tag with green ink. Stamp a row (see page 8) of three *Carved Flower* images along the bottom edge and below the tag top hole. Cut along the inner edge of the stamped rows with the wave scissors. Sponge the scallop edge of the two pieces with blue ink and heat set.

**3** Align the *Carved Flower* piece with the tag hole onto the blue stippled tag hole, then attach an eyelet (see page 6) into each top corner to secure the pieces together. Layer the *Carved Flower* bottom piece onto the bottom edge of the blue stippled tag and attach an eyelet into each bottom corner to secure both tags together.

**4** Lightly pencil a 2" square window centered on the blue portion of the tag. Place the tag on a cutting surface and use the knife to cut out the window. Sponge the window edges with blue and green inks and heat set. Lightly sand random areas of the tag. Place the photo centered behind the window and secure it with tape.

**5** Stipple the remaining blank tag green. Sponge the tag edges with blue ink and heat set. Place the top of this tag behind the window tag bottom, so ¾" extends beyond the bottom edge and glue in place so each end has a tag hole. Attach an eyelet near each corner of the window so all the pieces are secured together.

**6** Cut ten 7" lengths of gold floss. Hold five lengths together, thread them through one of the tag holes and pull the ends even. Slide a bead onto the floss next to the tag edge and glue in place. Repeat for the other tag hole. Glue a magnet at the top and bottom back of the tag.

# Ceramics

**W**orking with ceramics, tiles and terra cotta is more fun with rubber stamping!

# Embossed Clay Pot

**rubber stamps:**
  Design Elements
    Collection
    (swirl,
    diamond
    border)
  Fleur de Lis
gold permanent
  ink
**chalk inks:**
  Spanish Sand
  Painted Desert
  white
metallic embossing
  powder
burgundy acrylic
  paint
thin copper metal

6¼"x5½" terra
  cotta pot
22" length of 1½"
  wide wire mesh
  ribbon
liquid acrylic all-
  purpose sealer
foam sponges
1" wide foam
  brush
fine grain
  sandpaper
E6000® glue
embossing heat
  tool
tracing, transfer
  paper

**1** Use the foam brush to apply sealer (see page 5) to the inside and outside of the terra cotta pot; let dry. Lightly sponge (see page 7) white, tan and red inks randomly on the pot outside; let dry.

**2** Stamp the *Fleur de Lis* and the *Swirl* from the *Design Elements Collection* with gold ink randomly on the outside of the pot. While the ink is still wet, sprinkle embossing powder on top and heat set (see page 9); let dry. Stamp the *Diamond Border* from the *Design Elements Collection* with gold ink around the rim. Sprinkle embossing powder on each diamond and heat set; let dry.

## For other uses:

This pot is designed for decorative use only. If moisture seeps into terra cotta any stamping, painting and attached embellishments will be destroyed. To protect the pot for other uses, place a plastic liner inside. Plastic liners are available at most garden stores.

**3** Trace and transfer the triangle pattern (see page 13) to cut six copper metal triangles. Sponge each piece with burgundy paint and let dry. Lightly sand sections of each foil piece. Beginning with the wider end, roll one foil piece around the center of the metal mesh ribbon. Continue wrapping the foil until the point is wrapped to the backside. Glue the ribbon ends together and wrap a triangle over them. Evenly space and wrap two foil pieces around the ribbon on each side of the circle. Place the pot inside the ribbon circle and slide it upward to the rim's bottom edge. Glue the wrapped foil pieces to the pot sides and let dry.

# Terra Cotta Mosaic Vase

Leaf Whimsey rubber stamp
Evergreen chalk ink
Copper pigment ink
acrylic paints:
    metallic copper
    white
    green
two 6"x7½" terra cotta rose pots
20" length of ½" wide navy satin
    ribbon with sheer edges
liquid acrylic all-purpose sealer
metallic copper embroidery floss
1" wide foam brush
stipple brush
large sealable plastic bag
hammer
low temperature glue gun, glue
    sticks
embossing heat tool

**1** Apply sealer (see page 5) to the outside and inside of both pots; let dry.

**2** Stamp *Leaf Whimsey* with green ink repeatedly to cover the outside of one pot and heat set (see page 9). Stipple (see page 7) white, copper and green paint along the top and bottom of the pot; let dry. Apply sealer, let dry and set aside.

**3** Paint the other pot white and let dry. Add green paint to half of the pot and let dry. Stamp *Leaf Whimsey* with green and copper inks to cover the pot outside; let dry.

**4** Place the green and white pot into the plastic bag, seal it and use the hammer to break it into 1"-2" pieces. Remove the pieces and glue them in a mosaic pattern onto the first pot. Apply sealer to the entire pot and let dry.

**5** Cut two 22" lengths of floss, wrap them around the pot top and knot to secure. Make a shoestring bow (see page 13) with the ribbon and trim the tails to 2". Cut an 18" length of floss and wrap it around the center to completely cover the bow knot. Glue the bow to the floss knot on the pot. Spread the floss ends outward as shown.

## For other uses:

This vase makes a great catch-all for many bathroom items. Fill it with hand towels and washclothes for easy access. Or insert your hair brushes, combs and other accessories.

## Grape Leaf Terra Cotta Pot

### Why use sealer?

Acrylic all-purpose sealer is an important step in providing a surface for the ink to adhere. A coat of varnish applied to the pot after the stamping is complete protects the stamped surface.

*Grape Leaf Corner rubber stamp*
*chalk inks:*
  *Spanish Sand*
  *Brushed Sage*
  *Evergreen*
*green pigment ink*
*white acrylic paint*
*liquid acrylic all-purpose sealer*
*liquid clear gloss varnish*
*4½"x4" terra cotta pot*
*15½"x 1" strip of green burlap*
  *with frayed edges*
*16mm green rectangle acrylic*
  *rhinestone*
*20" length of thin metallic gold*
  *cord*
*20" length of metallic green*
  *embroidery floss*
*1" wide foam brush*
*stipple brush*
*tacky craft glue*
*low temperature glue gun, glue*
  *sticks*
*embossing heat tool*

**1** Apply sealer (see page 5) to the pot and let dry. Use the foam brush to paint the inside and outside of the pot white and let dry.

**2** Stamp *Grape Leaf Corner* with a combination of chalk inks randomly on the outside of the pot. Stipple (see page 7) green ink along the bottom and top edges of the pot. Heat set (see page 9) the pot outside, then immediately spray it with varnish and lightly brush it for a blended effect; let dry.

**3** Glue the burlap piece and wrap it around the pot rim.

**4** Wrap the gold cord and floss together around the rim several times and knot to secure. Trim the tails to 2"-3". Glue the rhinestone over the knot.

# Creative Fern Coaster

rubber stamps:
  Fern
  Leaf Whimsey
chalk inks:
  Painted Desert
  Espresso
pigment inks:
  copper
  black
copper embossing powder
X-acto® knife, cutting surface
tacky craft glue
embossing heat tool

**for each coaster:**
beige shrink plastic
twelve ¾" square white glazed
  mosaic tiles
3"x3" black matboard

**1** Stamp *Fern* onto the shrink plastic (see page 12) with a combination of the chalk inks. Use the knife to cut out a square, close to the stamped image. Follow the manufacturer's instructions to bake the shrink plastic. Allow it to cool completely.

**2** Sponge the shrink plastic edges (see page 7) with copper ink. Sprinkle copper embossing powder onto the wet ink and heat set (see page 9); let dry.

**3** Ink the raised areas of *Leaf Whimsey* with brown ink, then press a mosaic tile piece onto the inked stamp. Repeat, re-inking the stamp every third stamping. Heat set each tile piece; let dry.

**4** Glue the tile pieces along the edge of the black mat. Glue the shrink plastic piece in the center. Repeat to make a set of coasters.

# Domino Brooch

On the Metro Wall rubber
   stamp
Primary 5-Color Rainbow
   pigment inks
Blue Suede chalk ink
three ⅞"x1¾" dominoes
metallic copper
   embroidery floss
¾"x1¾" rectangle of white
   cardstock
buttons:
   ⅜" wide silver with
     rhinestone center
   ½" wide silver with
     rhinestone center
   ⅝" silver with ivory inset

glass beads:
   four 8mm red
   two 8mm copper tube
liquid clear matte varnish
1" wide foam brush
stipple brush
fine grain sandpaper
1½" long jewelry pin
foam sponge
low temperature glue gun,
   glue sticks
embossing heat tool

**1** Sponge (see page 7) a mixture of Rainbow inks onto the back of each domino. Stamp portions of *On the Metro Wall* onto each domino with blue ink and heat set (see page 9).

**2** Randomly stipple (see page 7) copper ink around the edges of each domino, sprinkle embossing powder on top of the wet ink and heat set. Lightly sand the edges of each domino.

**3** Glue the dominoes side-by-side onto the cardstock. Apply a coat of varnish over the dominoes and let dry. Apply a second coat and let dry.

**4** Thread a red, a copper tube and another red bead onto copper floss, then glue the beads in a column onto the cardstock along the left side of the dominoes. Continue to wrap the floss between each domino, thread the remaining beads onto the floss and glue them along the other end of the dominoes. Glue the buttons on top as shown. Glue the pin back to the brooch center top back.

# Domino Key Chain

rubber stamps:
   Scrollwork Scrapbook
     Set
Primary 5-Color
   Rainbow pigment inks
Blue Shadow chalk ink
⅞"x1¾" domino
thin silver metal:
   ⅞"x1¾" rectangle
   ⅜"x2" rectangle
⅜" wide silver button
   with rhinestone center

³⁄₁₆" wide silver eyelet,
   eyelet setting tools
¾" wide silver key ring
24-gauge silver wire
liquid clear gloss
   varnish
1" wide foam brush
fine grain sandpaper
low temperature glue
   gun, glue sticks
embossing heat tool

**1** Sponge (see page 7) a mixture of Rainbow inks onto the back of the domino. Stamp portions of a variety of stamps from the *Scrollwork Scrapbook Set* onto the domino with blue ink and heat set (see page 9).

**2** Apply a coat of varnish on the domino and let dry. Apply a second coat and let dry. Lightly sand the domino edges.

**3** Fold the narrow foil strip in half to form a ⅜"x1" piece and attach the eyelet (see page 6) ⅛" from the folded edge. Glue the other end behind the domino top so ½" extends beyond the edge. Cut a 7" length of wire and wrap it three times around the domino, gluing the ends at the back, then glue the remaining foil piece to the back of the domino. Trim the corners to the shape of the domino and sand to remove any sharp edges.

**4** Glue the button to the lower left corner of the domino. Thread the eyelet onto the key ring.

# Glass

The transparent nature of glass makes a spectacular surface for rubber stamping. Stamp directly onto the glass for a translucent effect or stamp on paper and insert it behind the glass for a 3-dimensional look. Yes, you can emboss on glass, too!

# Mini Candle Lamp

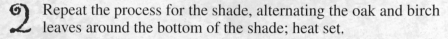

*Falling Leaves (set of 3) rubber stamps*
*permanent inks:*
  *green*
  *brown*
  *red*
*2"x2¼" frosted glass votive with*
  *ivory candle*
*3"x1¾" frosted glass shade with*
  *metal harp*
*embossing heat tool*

**1** Lightly ink the maple leaf from *Falling Leaves* with a combination of the three inks. Stamp the leaf onto the center of the candle base, rolling it slightly and firmly from left to right to form the complete image; heat set (see page 9).

**2** Repeat the process for the shade, alternating the oak and birch leaves around the bottom of the shade; heat set.

# Beaded Glass Bottle

*Fleur de Lis rubber stamp*
*Enchantment Petalpoint™ ink pad*
*embossing powders:*
  *bronze, clear*
*1⅜"x1⅜"x7¼" clear glass bottle with*
  *a cork stopper*

*glass beads:*
  *one 10mm green*
  *two 8mm copper embossed*
*24-gauge gold wire*
*liquid acrylic all-purpose sealer*
*½" wide paintbrush*
*needle nose pliers*
*embossing heat tool*

**1** Apply sealer (see page 5) to the bottle front to give the embossing powder a nonslick surface on which to cling. Pull out the green ink petal from the pad and sponge the bottle front. Sprinkle clear embossing powder on top and heat set (see page 9). Repeat the process two-three more times to achieve a thick coating.

**2** Sponge (see page 7) green ink onto the bottle front top, sprinkle a heavy coating of bronze powder on top and heat set. Repeat layering four-five times. While the final layer is still hot stamp *Fleur de Lis* fimly into the bronze mixture. Allow the mixture to cool beforc removing the stamp. Repeat the layering process near the bottom of the bottle front.

**3** Cut a 3-foot length of wire. Wrap the wire center around the bottle bottom three times, crisscrossing the ends at the back then bring the ends up and wrap them around the neck three times, twisting the ends tightly with the pliers.

**4** Cut an 18" length of wire, wrap the center around the neck crisscrossing the ends at the front, then coil each end around the paintbrush handle. Remove the handle and wrap a bead onto each end. Wrap the remaining bead onto a 6" length of wire and wrap the end around the cork stopper.

# Holiday Glass Ornaments

rubber stamps:
  Fancy Ornament
  Design Elements Collection
Embossing Magic™
Frosted White pigment ink
embossing powders:
  white
  silver
clear glass ornaments:
  3" wide round
  2¾"x4" teardrop
24" of ¼" wide white sheer ribbon
liquid acrylic all-purpose sealer
1" wide foam brush
pencil with new eraser
2 cloth hot pads or a kitchen towel
embossing heat tool

**1** Wash the ornaments with hot, soapy water, rinse; let dry thoroughly. To prepare the glass surface for stamping, apply a coat of sealer (see page 5) to each ornament and let dry. Rub *Embossing Magic*™ (see page 6) over each ornament.

**2** Mix an equal amount of white and silver embossing powders. Gently place the teardrop ornament on its side on a hot pad or kitchen towel. Stamp *Fancy Ornament* on the center front with white ink, carefully rolling the stamp from side-to-side along the curved surface. Sprinkle the embossing powder mixture onto the wet ink and heat set (see page 9). Avoid overheating the glass to prevent it from cracking.

**3** Gently place the round ornament on the remaining hot pad. Stamp the *Swirl* and *Star* from the *Design Elements Collection* evenly spaced on one side of the ornament. Sprinkle the embossing ink powder mixture onto the wet ink and heat set. Dip the pencil eraser tip into the ink pad and press it onto the ornament between the *Swirls* and *Stars*. Sprinkle embossing powder on top and heat set. Allow the side to completely cool, then turn the ornament over and repeat the stamping and embossing process until the entire surface of the ornament is embellished.

**4** Cut the ribbon in half. With one length, insert the center through the ornament top hanger, then tie a shoestring bow (see page 13) with a 2½" center loop, two 1¼" side loops and two 1½" tails. Repeat for the remaining ornament. Trim each bow tail at an angle.

## "On the Metro Wall" Candle Holder

*On the Metro Wall rubber*
*   stamp*
*chalk inks:*
*   Blue Suede*
*   Lavender Flower*
*   Pacific Horizon*
*copper pigment ink*
*copper embossing powder*
*3¼"x3¼"x3¼" glass candle*
*   holder*
*four 1½"x1¼" rectangles of*
*   ivory cardstock*
*liquid acrylic all-purpose*
*   sealer*
*foam sponges*
*E6000® glue or Ultimate*
*   Glue®*
*embossing heat tool*

**1** Wash the candle holder with hot, soapy water, rinse and let dry completely. Apply a coat of sealer (see page 5) on the inside and outside of the holder; let dry. Randomly stamp (see page 8) *On the Metro Wall* with Blue Suede ink on each side of the holder and heat set (see page 9). Avoid overheating the glass to prevent it from cracking. Sponge (see page 7) lavender and Pacific Horizon inks along the inside of the candle holder; heat set.

**2** Sponge each cardstock rectangle with copper ink. Sprinkle embossing powder on top of the wet ink on each

rectangle and heat set. Sponge each rectangle once more, sprinkle embossing powder on top and heat set for a second layer. Reheat one rectangle and stamp a portion of *On the Metro Wall* onto it while it is still hot with copper ink. Repeat for each rectangle and let cool. Apply a coat of sealer on the inside and outside of the candle holder; let dry.

**3** Glue an embossed rectangle onto each side of the candle holder.

*Square Leaf Fern*
  *rubber stamp*
*Pinwheel Petalpoint™*
  *ink pad*
*silver pigment ink*
*embossing powders:*
  *silver*
  *clear*
*embossing marker*
*4"x3½" clear glass*
  *flowerpot*
*liquid acrylic all-*
  *purpose sealer*
*embossing heat tool*

**1** Wash the flowerpot with hot, soapy water, rinse and let dry thoroughly. Apply a coat of sealer (see page 5) onto the flowerpot outside; let dry.

**2** Randomly stamp (see page 8) *Square Leaf Fern* onto the outside of the pot with green ink and heat set (see page 9). Avoid overheating the glass to prevent it from cracking.

**3** Sponge (see page 7) the entire pot below the rim with blue ink. Randomly sprinkle clear embossing powder onto the wet ink and heat set.

**4** Sponge 1" wide bands of light green and blue around the pot rim. Randomly sprinkle clear embossing powder onto the wet ink and heat set. Apply a coat of sealer onto the outside of the pot; let dry.

**5** Sponge the bottom edge and top rim with silver ink. Sprinkle silver embossing powder on top of the wet ink and heat set. Use the embossing marking to draw lines between the green and blue sections along the rim as shown. Sprinkle silver embossing powder on top and heat set.

# Glass Brush Holder

rubber stamps:
  Lettre
  Baroque Vine
  Corinthian Column
  Captain's Walk (ironwork
    border)
black permanent ink
metallic gold pigment ink
chalk inks:
  Espresso
  Spanish Sand
gold embossing powder
3¾"x7" glass vase
brown kraft paper
15"x5½" ivory cardstock

liquid clear gloss varnish
liquid acrylic all-purpose
  sealer
decoupage glue
X-acto® knife, cutting
  surface
paper towel
cotton swabs
1" wide foam brush
stipple brush
clear adhesive tape
embossing heat tool

**1** Apply sealer (see page 5) to the outside of the vase and let dry. Stamp *Lettre, Baroque Vine, Corinthian Column* and *Captain's Walk* with a mixture of the inks onto the outer surface of the glass vase. (If it smudges, wipe the ink off and re-stamp.) Heat set (see page 9) the stamped impressions and let dry. Apply a light coat of sealer on the outside and let dry.

**2** Optional: Stipple (see page 7) one side of the cardstock with brown ink and let dry. Stamp *Lettre* randomly onto the other side with tan ink and let dry. Insert the cardstock into the vase with the lettering facing through the glass vase and secure the ends with tape.

**3** Tear 1"-1½" squares and rectangles of brown paper. Apply decoupage glue to the paper pieces and place 1½" along the inner and outer vase mouth then apply a second coat of decoupage glue; let dry. Apply a coat of varnish onto the decoupaged area and let dry.

**4** Stamp the gold ink pad directly onto the vase rim. Sprinkle gold embossing powder onto the wet ink and heat set.

# Wood

Create heirloom gifts for your family and friends by rubber stamping on wood. This natural surface makes a perfect canvas for any stamping technique. Apply an acrylic varnish to the completed project for a permanent finish.

# Contemplation Decorative Frame

rubber stamps:
  Filigree Corner
  Texture Water
  Contemplation
  Captain's Walk
    (ironwork border)
chalk inks:
  Blue Suede
  Espresso
  Painted Desert
pigment inks:
  Black Picture Perfect
  gold
gold embossing powder
decorative chalks:
  purple
  red
  blue

6"x8" ivory paper
8"x10" unfinished wood
  frame with 4⅝"x6½"
  opening
chalk applicators
1" wide foam brush
stipple brush
liquid acrylic all-
  purpose sealer
liquid clear gloss
  varnish
X-acto® knife, cutting
  surface
fine grain sandpaper
foam sponges
clean soft cloth
embossing heat tool

**1** Apply sealer (see page 5) to the frame and let dry. Sand the frame front and sides; wipe the surface with the cloth to remove all dust. Randomly sponge (see page 8) blue and red inks onto different areas of the wood surface and heat set (see page 9).

**2** Randomly stamp *Filigree Corner, Texture Water* and *Captain's Walk* onto the frame front with gold ink. Sprinkle gold embossing powder on top of some of the wet ink and heat set, then heat set the un-embossed ink areas. Lightly sand sections around the frame to create a distressed look. Spray the frame with varnish and let dry.

**3** Randomly stipple (see page 7) gold ink onto the ivory paper and heat set. Stamp *Filigree Corner, Texture Water* and *Captain's Walk* around the edges of the ivory paper with gold ink and heat set.

**4** Stamp *Filigree Corner* near the upper left and lower right corners with brown ink. Stamp *Contemplation* in the center with black ink and heat set. Randomly chalk *Contemplation* with purple, red and blue.

**5** Spray a coat of varnish over the ivory rectangle and let dry thoroughly. Glue the ivory sheet to the back the frame.

# Gold Leaf Jewelry Box

*Leaf Whimsey rubber stamp*
*metallic gold pigment ink*
*gold embossing powder*
*acrylic paint:*
  *metallic copper*
  *burgundy*
*8 1/8"x6 1/2"x4" rounded top unfinished*
  *wood box with brass hinges &*
  *front clasp*
*small Phillips head screwdriver*
*1" wide foam brush*
*stipple brush*
*liquid acrylic all-purpose sealer*
*fine grain sandpaper*
*clean soft cloth*
*embossing heat tool*

**1** Use the screwdriver to remove the hinges and clasps from the box; set them aside.

**2** Apply sealer (see page 5) to the box and let dry. Lightly sand the box and wipe clean. To create texture on the box, ramdomly stipple (see page 7) gold ink onto the surface, sprinkle gold embossing powder on top of the wet ink and heat set (see page 9).

**3** Paint the entire outside surface of the box burgundy and let dry. Brush on copper paint to accent the edges and various sections; let dry.

**4** Randomly stamp *Leaf Whimsey* onto the box with gold ink. Sprinkle gold embossing powder onto various areas of wet ink and heat set; then heat set the entire surface of the box. Apply sealer to the box and let dry.

**5** Re-assemble the hinges and clasps onto the box.

# Scrollworks Frame

rubber stamps:
  Scrollwork Scrapbook
    Set
  Lettre
Espresso Chalk Ink
metallic pigment inks:
  gold
  silver
  copper
embossing powders:
  gold
  silver
  copper
ivory acrylic paint
6½"x8½" unfinished
  wood frame with a
  3⅝"x5¾" opening
1" wide foam brush
stipple brush
4"x6" photograph
liquid acrylic all-purpose
  sealer
fine grain sandpaper
clean soft cloth
embossing heat tool

**1** Apply sealer (see page 5) to the frame and let dry. Lightly sand the frame and wipe clean. Thin the ivory paint in a 1:1 ratio with water. Use the foam brush to lightly apply it to the entire wood surface so the grain shows through; let dry completely.

**2** Stamp *Lettre* with brown and gold inks multiple times to cover the frame (see page 10); heat set (see page 9).

**3** Stamp *Corner Swirl* from the *Scrollwork Scrapbook Set* onto the lower right corner of the frame with gold ink. While the ink is still wet, sprinkle the ink with gold, silver and copper embossing powders and heat set. Stamp various images onto the frame, repeating the inking and embossing process.

**4** Insert the photo into the frame and secure with the frame pegs.

# Clock Face Switch Plate & Tissue Box Cover

rubber stamps:
  London Calling
  Clock & Hands (set of 3)
chalk inks:
  Spanish Sand
  Espresso
black dye ink
3"x4³⁄₈" unfinished wood switch plate cover
5"x5"x6¹⁄₈" unfinished wood tissue box
1" wide foam brush
liquid clear matte varnish
foam sponges
fine grain sandpaper
embossing heat tool

**1** Lightly sand the switch plate cover and the tissue box. Apply a coat of varnish (see page 5) to each piece and let dry.

**2** Sponge (see page 7) tan ink onto the switch plate and tissue box, then sponge brown and black inks around the edges of each piece. Sponge brown onto the switch opening on the plate and around the opening of the box cover and heat set (see page 9).

**3** Stamp the *Clock* from the *Clock & Hands* set onto the switch plate center with brown and black inks. Randomly stamp (see page 8) the *Clock, Hands* and *London Calling* onto the switch plate and on each side and top of the tissue box cover with brown and black inks; heat set each piece and let dry thoroughly.

**4** Apply a coat of varnish over the entire switch plate and tissue box cover; let dry. Mount the switch plate over the light switch using the screws to secure.

46

# Dream with Faith Box

rubber stamps:
  Dream with Faith
  Daisy
  Bumble Bee
  Four Point Flourish
  Filigree Corner
chalk inks:
  Painted Desert
  Espresso
black dye ink
clear embossing ink
gold embossing powder
$5\frac{1}{4}$"x$3\frac{3}{4}$"x$3\frac{1}{4}$"
  unfinished wood box
  with lid; brass hinges
  and clasp; and a
  $3\frac{1}{2}$"x$1\frac{7}{8}$" frame
  opening on the lid
$3\frac{1}{2}$"x$1\frac{7}{8}$" rectangle of
  $\frac{1}{16}$" thick basswood
gold micro beads
liquid clear gloss
  varnish
1" wide foam brush
tacky craft glue
toothpick
foam sponges
fine grain sandpaper
clean soft cloth
embossing heat tool

**1** Lightly sand the box and wipe clean. Apply a coat of varnish (see page 5) to the box, lid and basswood rectangle; let dry.

**2** Sponge (see page 7) red ink onto the basswood rectangle and wipe off the excess ink for a uniform look; let dry.

**3** Stamp *Dream with Faith* and *Bumble Bee* onto the basswood rectangle with black ink; let dry thoroughly. Mask (see page 9) off the *Bumble Bee* then stamp *Daisy* onto the right side as shown. Remove the mask and heat set.

**4** Sponge embossing ink onto the basswood edges, sprinkle gold embossing powder on top of the wet ink and heat set. Apply a coat of varnish onto the basswood and let dry.

**5** Ink the *Four Point Flourish* stamp with brown ink. Press it onto the front left corner of the lid top, then wrap the extending portion down onto the front side, lift up and press the other stamp edge onto the left side. Repeat for each corner of the lid. Turn the stamp on point and stamp a full image centered onto the box front; heat set.

**6** Stamp *Filigree Corner* with brown ink onto each side of the box front and back. Re-ink the stamp, turn it pointing downward and stamp it onto each side and centered on the box back; heat set. Apply a coat of varnish to the box and lid; let dry.

**7** Apply a thin line of glue along the top of the bottom ridge around the box. Press a line of gold micro beads onto the ridge. Use another toothpick to press the beads into the glue and straighten the line and let dry. Glue the basswood rectangle centered in the opening on the lid top.

# Papier Mâché

**P**apier mâché offers a world of possibilities with rubber stamping. You can stamp directly onto the surface (after sealing it with a liquid acrylic all-purpose sealer), or paint it first, then stamp on it. Either way, you'll love the results!

# Antique Keepsake Box

rubber stamps:
  Framed Swirl
  Ancient Text
chalk inks:
  Painted Desert
  Spanish Sand
  Pink Porcelain
5"x4½"x2½" ivory papier
  mâché polygon box with
  lid
2½" square of ivory
  cardstock
2¼" square of pink mulberry
  paper
28" length of 1" wide
  gathered ivory lace trim
⅝" wide silver/ivory button
metallic embroidery flosss:
  rose
  copper
  burgundy
stipple brush
foam sponges
deckle pattern-edge scissors
low temperature glue gun,
  glue sticks
embossing heat tool

## Papier Mâché tip:

The surface of papier mâché is usually uneven, so stamping on it creates an uneven image. Distressing and aging techniques can be used with a papier mâché surface to highlight its unique quality and to hide any imperfect stamping!

1 Remove the lid from the box. Randomly sponge (see page 8) the three chalk inks onto the box and lid, then use the brush to stipple the edges; heat set (see page 9).

2 Glue the lace trim in a spiral around the lid beginning at the outer edge and working inward.

3 Stamp *Framed Swirl* onto the cardstock with red and tan inks; heat set. Use the deckle scissors to cut out the stamped image into a 2⅜" square. Stipple the edges with the inks and heat set. Turn the stamped square on point and glue it centered on the mulberry square. Glue the piece centered on the lid over the lace.

4 Stamp *Ancient Text* with red ink on each side of the box and heat set.

5 Cut the floss into 9" lengths. Fold them in half and glue them to the bottom tip of the stamped square on the lid. Glue the button to the fiber folds as shown.

# Believe Dreamcatcher

rubber stamps:
  Minnie
  Zebra Butterfly
  Believe
chalk inks:
  Blue Shadow
  Pacific Horizon
  Lavender Flower
silver pigment ink
silver embossing powder
violet acrylic paint
3½" round papier mâché ornament
beads:
  one 16mm round purple/silver
    paisley print
  seven 3mm light blue glass pony
  two 3mm clear glass pony
  one 3mm light green glass pony
1¼" wide silver earring hoop

22-gauge silver wire
black with multi-colored metallic
  strands embroidery floss
1⅛"x1¾" white tag with scallop-
  edge top
1" wide foam brush
stipple brush
tacky craft glue
scrap paper
foam sponge
X-acto® knife
wire cutters
embossing heat tool

**1** Remove the hanger from the ornament. Paint the ornament violet and let dry. Stipple (see page 7) lavender and Pacific Horizon inks onto the front and back of the ornament. Stamp *Minnie* onto the ornament center front with Blue Shadow and heat set (see page 9). Stamp *Minnie* once more on scrap paper, cut it out and place it over the stamped image on the ornament to mask it off.

**2** Mask *Minnie* then randomly stamp (see page 8) *Zebra Butterfly* onto the ornament front and back with lavender and Pacific Horizon inks; heat set. Use the tip of the X-acto® knife to make a small hole in the center bottom of the ornament,

then two on top, centered 1¼" apart. Roll the ornament on its side along the silver ink pad, sprinkle with silver embossing powder and heat set. Make sure to keep the holes open.

**3** Use the direct-to-paper technique to apply silver ink onto both sides of the tag and heat set. Stipple lavender and Blue Shadow inks onto the tag front. Sponge silver ink on the edges, sprinkle embossing powder on top and heat set. Stamp *believe* onto the tag with Blue Shadow ink and heat set.

**4** Cut a 7" length of wire. Bend the wire in half to form a loop, then hold the wire ends together and insert a green and blue bead onto the ends and slide them up to 1" below the loop top; twist once below and above the beads to secure them in place. Slide three beads onto each single wire end (blue, clear, blue), then place a dot of glue at the wire end and insert it into each top hole. Cut two 1" wire lengths. Wrap one length around each wire twist above and below the top two beads.

**5** Cut a 1" length of wire, bend in half and twist the ends to form a ¼" loop. Glue the ends into the ornament bottom hole. Cut a 2½" length of wire. Thread one end through the ornament bottom loop and twist to secure. Slide a blue pony, the paisley bead, then the remaining blue pony onto the wire length. Loop the wire end onto the earring loop and twist to secure, then back up through the three beads to hide the wire end.

**6** Cut ten 12" lengths of floss. Fold one in half, wrap the loop around the earring bottom and pull the ends through the loop to secure it to the earring (see page 13, Threading a tag, for the technique diagram). Repeat for each remaining floss length. Cut a 5" length of floss, loop it around the top right wire section below the beads, then thread one end through the tag hole and knot the ends together.

# Papier Mâché Box

Design Elements Collection
    rubber stamps
Espresso chalk ink
copper pigment ink
copper embossing powder
3"x6"x6" papier mâché box
five 1¼" wide unfinished wood
    knobs
15" of ⅝" wide copper sheer
    ribbon
gold thread
"Love" and "Romance" Paper
    Pizazz® Romantic Embossed
    Paper Charms
acrylic paints:
    gold
    copper
liquid clear gloss varnish
foam sponge
1" wide foam brush
fine grain sandpaper
¹⁄₁₆" hole punch
tacky craft glue
embossing heat tool

**1** Remove the lid from the box. Use the foam brush to paint the inside and outsides of the box and lid gold (see page 10); let dry. Rinse the brush, then paint each knob copper and let dry.

**2** Stamp the *Diamonds & Dots* border from the *Design Elements Collection* in five rows on one side of the box with brown ink. While the ink is still wet, use the sponge to lightly wipe the stamped images to smear them until they appear faded. Heat set (see page 9) the box side. Repeat the process for each of the remaining box sides.

**3** Randomly stamp (see page 8) *Flourish* from the *Design Elements Collection* onto the lid top with brown ink. While the ink is still wet, use the sponge to lightly wipe the stamped images to smear them until they appear faded. Heat set the lid top. Use the direct-to-paper technique to apply copper ink along the lid sides, sprinkle copper embossing ink on top of the wet ink and heat set. Use the direct-to-paper technique to randomly apply copper ink on the box bottom edges and on the lid top; heat set.

**4** Lightly sand the box sides, edges and lid for a distressed look. Lightly sand the knobs. Spray the box and lid with varnish; let dry.

**5** Glue the flat side of a knob to each bottom corner of the box, then the remaining knob centered on the lid top; let dry. Cut two 5" lengths of thread. Cut out each embossed paper charm, then punch a hole into the top of each charm. Thread a thread length onto each charm, wrap the thread around the lid knob and knot the ends to secure. Wrap the ribbon around the knob and tie it into a shoestring bow (see page 13) with 1½" loops and 3" tails. Tie a knot near each tail end, then cut an inverted "V" into each tail end.

## Papier Mâché tip:

**P**apier mâché is an inexpensive material and is available in most craft stores in a variety of shapes and sizes. It's a perfect choice for gifts!

# Vellum

Vellum is ideal for rubber stamping, as it's translucent quality allows the image to merge onto the background or show through from the back. It takes longer for ink to dry on vellum, so take care to prevent smearing before it's dry.

# Carved Icon Card

rubber stamps:
  Carved Shell
  Carved Heart
  Carved Star
  Carved Flower
chalk inks:
  Lavender Flower
  Spanish Sand
  Painted Desert
  Pacific Horizon
ten $\frac{1}{8}$" silver eyelets
eyelet setting tools
Paper Pizazz® vellums:
  pastel ivory
  white
ivory paper:
  $4\frac{3}{4}$"x$6\frac{3}{4}$" rectangle
  four $1\frac{1}{8}$" squares
$5\frac{1}{2}$"x$7\frac{1}{2}$" rectangle of tan
    corrugated paper
$5\frac{1}{8}$"x7" blank white card
metallic silver embroidery floss
3 ivory pony beads
sewing needle with large eye
Victorian pattern-edge scissors
glue stick
clear adhesive tape
embossing heat tool

**1** Stamp the following onto the white vellum (see page 10): *Carved Flower* with lavender ink, *Carved Star* with tan ink, *Carved Heart* with red ink and *Carved Shell* with blue ink. Heat set (see page 9) each and trim around each to form $1\frac{5}{8}$" squares. Glue an ivory paper square centered behind each stamped vellum square. Attach an eyelet (see page 6) into each top and bottom of each vellum square; set them aside.

**2** Stamp in the same sequence as listed in step 1 to create two rows of imprints along the left and right sides of the ivory paper rectangle and heat set. Place a $4\frac{1}{2}$"x$6\frac{1}{2}$" rectangle of ivory vellum centered on the paper rectangle and secure the pieces together with an eyelet centered at the top and bottom edges.

**3** Thread the needle with floss, insert it into the bottom eyelet from the back to the front and tape the floss end to the paper back. Continue with the needle, inserting it through the shell square front in the bottom eyelet, onto the back and out the front of the top eyelet. Then, thread a bead onto the floss and repeat the process to attach the heart, star and flower squares. Insert the other end of the floss through the top paper eyelet and tape the end at the back. To hold the squares in place, place a dab of glue behind each one.

**4** Trim the corrugated paper with the Victorian scissors. Glue the ivory piece centered on the corrugated rectangle, then glue the entire piece to the card front.

# Depth in Creation

rubber stamps:
  Creation Collage
  Four Point Flourish
Espresso chalk ink
Copper pigment ink
copper embossing powder
decorative chalks:
  peach
  brown
  yellow
10"x10" white spiral-bound journal
Paper Pizazz® papers:
  6½"x6" rectangle of white vellum
  1½" square of metallic gold
  12" square of brown diamonds
  4"x3½" rectangle of cream paper
  4¾"x4¼" rectangle of cream paper
7"x6½" of burgundy cork-textured paper
tan fiber
metallic embroidery floss:
  burgundy
  copper
deckle pattern-edge scissors
¼" hole punch
X-acto® knife, cutting surface
foam adhesive tape
glue stick
embossing heat tool

**1** Stamp *Creation Collage* with brown ink on both cream paper rectangles; heat set (see page 9) each piece. Set the smaller rectangle aside. Trim the edges of the larger rectangle with deckle scissors. Sponge (see page 7) the edges with copper ink, sprinkle copper embossing powder on top of the wet ink and heat set.

**2** Place the larger stamped rectangle on a cutting surface and use the knife to cut out the section within the arch image, leaving the hands. Chalk the edges peach and brown and the arch yellow. Chalk inside the arch section on the other stamped image.

**3** Glue the smaller stamped rectangle centered on the back of the white vellum so the image shows through. Use foam tape at the corners to attach the larger stamped rectangle centered on top of the vellum with the arches aligned to reveal the uncut version behind the vellum.

**4** Place the burgundy cork texture paper on the cutting surface and use the ruler and knife to cut out a 6"x5½" section from the center to foam a frame. Glue the frame to the vellum rectangle.

**5** Trim the edges of the gold paper with the deckle scissors. Stamp the *Four Point Flourish* in the gold square center with copper ink, then sponge the edges. Sprinkle copper embossing powder onto the wet ink and heat set. Cut three strands each of fiber and floss to 5"–7" lengths. Hold the ends of each strand even and tape them to the back of the gold diamond bottom point. Use foam tape to attach the gold diamond to the upper left corner of the vellum frame as shown.

**6** Tear an 8½"x9" rectangle of brown diamonds paper. Remove the journal front cover from the spiral binding and glue the diamonds rectangle turned on point on the cover top. Turn the cover over and use the punch to punch holes through the pre-punched holes in the cover. Glue the vellum frame centered on the cover. Re-attach the cover onto the spiral binding.

*T*o remove the journal cover: Locate where the spiral binding comes together. On some journals, this will be between the back cover and the pages. On others, this will be between the front and back covers. Gently pull apart the binding and remove the cover. Occasionally, you will need to remove all of the pages as well so you can remove the cover. When you're done, simply replace the covers and pages in the reverse of how you removed them.

# Southwest Vellum Card

rubber stamps:
  Southwest Border
  Gecko
chalk inks:
  Spanish Sand
  Espresso
  Painted Desert
gold pigment ink
embossing powders:
  gold
  copper
6" square blank ivory card
Paper Pizazz® ivory vellum
2¼"x6" rectangle of burgundy
  handmade paper
metallic embroidery floss:
  burgundy
  gold
  copper
deckle pattern-edge scissors
stipple brush
foam sponge
metal ruler
tacky craft glue
glue stick
embossing heat tool

**1** Randomly stamp (see page 8) *Gecko* on the card front square using combinations of the chalk inks, then heat set (see page 9). Trim the card edges with the deckle scissors. Sponge (see page 7) the edges with gold ink, sprinkle copper embossing powder on top of the wet ink and heat set.

**2** Cut a 5½" square of vellum. Center the vellum on the card front and glue only the left side.

**3** Hold the ruler near the right long edge of the handmade paper and tear along the edge. Stamp two images of *Southwest Border* with gold ink centered in a column on the handmade paper, sprinkle gold embossing powder on top of the wet ink and

heat set. Stipple the left edge with gold ink. Glue the handmade paper to the card front to cover the glued vellum edge with the left edges even.

**4** Cut a 2¼"x3" rectangle of ivory vellum. Stamp a gold *Southwest Border* in the center, sprinkle gold embossing powder on top and heat set. Trim the edges with the deckle scissors. Sponge the edges with gold ink, sprinkle gold embossing powder on top and heat set.

**5** Cut ten 2"–4" lengths of floss and use the tacky glue to attach them centered behind the stamp on the embossed vellum rectangle.

# Vellum Pyramid Box

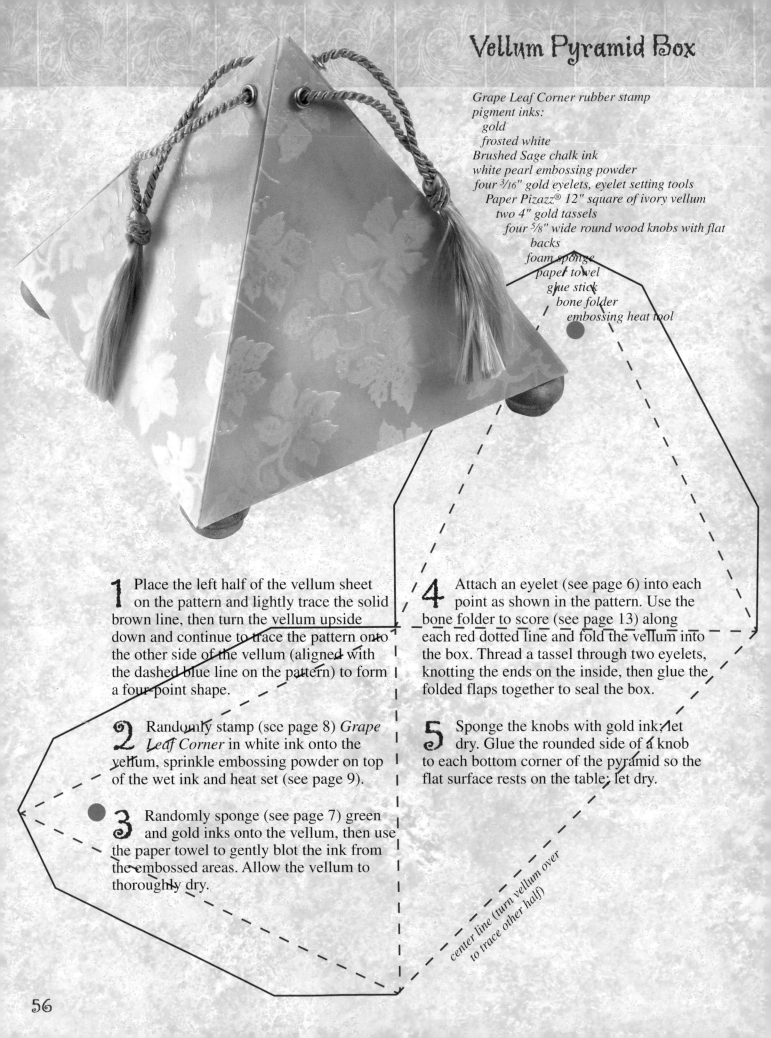

Grape Leaf Corner rubber stamp
pigment inks:
  gold
  frosted white
Brushed Sage chalk ink
white pearl embossing powder
four $^{3}/_{16}$" gold eyelets, eyelet setting tools
Paper Pizazz® 12" square of ivory vellum
two 4" gold tassels
four $^{5}/_{8}$" wide round wood knobs with flat
  backs
foam sponge
paper towel
glue stick
bone folder
embossing heat tool

**1** Place the left half of the vellum sheet on the pattern and lightly trace the solid brown line, then turn the vellum upside down and continue to trace the pattern onto the other side of the vellum (aligned with the dashed blue line on the pattern) to form a four-point shape.

**2** Randomly stamp (see page 8) *Grape Leaf Corner* in white ink onto the vellum, sprinkle embossing powder on top of the wet ink and heat set (see page 9).

**3** Randomly sponge (see page 7) green and gold inks onto the vellum, then use the paper towel to gently blot the ink from the embossed areas. Allow the vellum to thoroughly dry.

**4** Attach an eyelet (see page 6) into each point as shown in the pattern. Use the bone folder to score (see page 13) along each red dotted line and fold the vellum into the box. Thread a tassel through two eyelets, knotting the ends on the inside, then glue the folded flaps together to seal the box.

**5** Sponge the knobs with gold ink; let dry. Glue the rounded side of a knob to each bottom corner of the pyramid so the flat surface rests on the table; let dry.

center line (turn vellum over to trace other half)

# Jar of Bugs Shadow Box

rubber stamps:
  Mason Jar
  Bee
chalk inks:
  Lavender Flower
  Pacific Horizon
silver pigment ink
silver embossing powder
two ³/₁₆" silver eyelets,
  eyelet setting tools
plum handmade paper
white paper
Paper Pizazz® white vellum

white matboard
24-gauge silver wire
foam sponge
X-acto® knife, cutting
  surface
metal ruler
masking tape
decoupage glue
tacky craft glue
foam sponge
wire cutters
embossing heat tool

**1** To create the front and back of the shadow box, cut two 4¼"x6¼" rectangles of matboard. Cut a 3"x5" window in the center of one rectangle. For the shadow box sides, cut two 1"x6¼" and two 1"x4¼" strips of matboard. Glue the matboard strips to the sides, top and bottom of the window matboard piece. Glue the edges to the other matboard piece. Use masking tape to secure the edges until the glue is dry then remove the tape.

**2** Tear the plum paper into 2"-3" squares. Apply decoupage glue to the back of one piece and press it onto the box. Repeat, overlapping the edges to cover the entire outer surface and let dry. Sponge (see page 7) silver ink around the window edges and heat set (see page 9). Cut two 5¼" and two 3½" lengths of wire. Bend each in a slightly wavy shape, place them around the window and glue the ends in place at each corner.

**3** Stamp *Bee* onto white paper twice with lavender and twice with blue ink. Cut around the contour of each. Sponge the edge of each piece with silver, sprinkle embossing powder on top of the wet ink and heat set. Stamp *Bee* two times onto vellum with lavender ink and two times with blue ink and heat set. Cut out the body and wings of each stamped bee. Glue the bee body to a corresponding paper bee color then bend the wings slightly upward. Repeat for each bee. Glue a bee to each corner facing into the window as shown.

**4** Stamp *Mason Jar* onto vellum with silver ink, sprinkle embossing powder on top and heat set. Cut around the outer edge of the imprint, leaving ¼" on each side and ½" on the top and bottom. Place it on white paper and trace around the edge then cut out the paper shape.

**6** Randomly stamp *Bee* with lavender in the center of the cardboard jar shape and let dry. Randomly stamp *Bee* with blue onto the vellum jar within the lines and let dry. Layer the vellum piece over the cardstock and attach an eyelet (see page 6) at the top and bottom to secure them together.

**7** Cut two 2" wire lengths. Thread one length through the top eyelet, fold in half and glue the ends centered inside the window top. Repeat the process for the bottom eyelet.

# Metal

believe dream

aspire to BE

**M**etal takes rubber stamping into a whole new dimension. You can stamp, emboss or burnish designs into the material with spectacular results! Once you start, you won't stop with this fun surface.

# Foil Fern Journal

rubber stamps:
  Feather Fern
  Falling Leaves (set of 3)
pigment inks:
  silver
  gold
dark brown acrylic paint
8"x6" black spiral-bound
  journal
thin silver metal:
  one 3⅛"x4¾" rectangle
  four 1½" squares
white mulberry paper
7"x5" white matboard frame
  with 3½"x5½" opening
fine grain sandpaper
decoupage glue
bone folder
stipple brush
½" wide paintbrush
kitchen towel or craft foam
low temperature glue gun,
  glue sticks
embossing heat tool

**1** Randomly stamp (see page 8) *Falling Leaves* on the journal cover with silver ink and heat set (see page 9).

**2** Stamp *Feather Fern* on the metal rectangle back with any ink then place the metal piece on top of a towel or craft foam. Use the bone folder to press along the stamped imprint to create an embossed effect. Turn the metal so the embossed side is face up. Apply brown paint on and around the imprint, making sure to get it into the cracks and heat set. Use sandpaper to scratch off the paint on the imprint top and to add texture as shown. Stipple (see page7) gold ink on top of the sanded paint.

**3** Repeat step 2 with one of the *Falling Leaves* to stamp each of the four metal squares. Cut out each stamped leaf into a diamond shape.

**4** Tear the mulberry paper into ¾"x4" strips. Apply decoupage glue to the back of one piece and press it onto the frame, wrapping the edges around the sides. Repeat to cover the entire frame. Apply a coat of decoupage glue over the entire frame and let dry. Sponge silver ink to the inner and outer edges of the frame. Stipple gold and silver on the mulberry paper.

**5** Glue a metal diamond onto each corner of the frame. Glue the frame centered on the journal cover, then glue the embossed fern centered inside the frame.

On the Metro Wall rubber stamp
pigment inks:
    gold
      black
       purple
      permanent inks:
        black
        brown
        gold
      metallic embossing powders:
        gold
        copper
        silver
      $3\frac{1}{2}"x2\frac{1}{4}"x\frac{3}{4}"$ tin box with
        hinged lid
        three $\frac{3}{4}"$ square ivory ceramics
        tiles
buttons:
    one $1\frac{1}{4}"x1\frac{1}{4}"$ triangle with
      rhinestones
    one $\frac{5}{8}"$ wide ivory round with brass
      inset
liquid acrylic all-purpose sealer
$\frac{1}{2}"$ wide paintbrush
E6000® glue or Ultimate Glue®
foam sponge
embossing heat tool

**1** Open the lid (or remove it) and place it face up. Apply a coat of sealer (see page 5) to the lid and box; let dry. Sponge (see page 7) the lid with gold ink. Sprinkle a mix of metallic embossing powders on the lid and heat set (see page 9). Cover the lid again with gold ink and metallic embossing powders and heat set. Repeat one or two more times to achieve a thick embossed layer. While the last layer is still hot, stamp *On the Metro Wall* with black ink and allow to cool before removing the stamp. (If you're not happy with the results, add another layer of embossing powders and try again.)

**2** Use the paintbrush to apply gold ink between the stamped squares on the lid, sprinkle gold embossing powder on top of the wet ink and heat set.

**3** Turn the box bottom up. Sponge the box sides and bottom with gold ink. Sprinkle a mix of embossing powders on the sides and bottom and heat set. Limit the embossing to one layer to allow for opening and closing of the lid.

**4** Ink a portion of the stamp with purple ink and stamp a ceramic tile. Repeat with different portions of the stamp to achieve different patterns on the tiles; let dry. Lightly brush brown and gold inks onto each tile to create an antique effect; let dry.

**5** Apply a coat of sealer to the box and lid; let dry. Glue the tiles and buttons to the lid as shown.

# Leaf Dream Vase

rubber stamps:
  Aspire to BE
  Believe
  Dream
  Leaf Whimsey
pigment inks:
  black
  silver
Evergreen chalk ink
burgundy acrylic paint
embossing powders:
  silver
  black
3⅞"x3⅞"x8" tin vase
thin copper metal:
  one 3"x5" rectangle
  six ⅜"x2" strips
  one ¾"x2" strip

2¼"x4½" cardstock:
  cream
  black
  tan fiber
metallic embroidery
  flosss:
  burgundy
  copper
fine grain sandpaper
X-acto® knife, cutting
  surface
½" wide paintbrush
E6000® glue or
  Ultimate Glue®
embossing heat tool

**1** Trim each cardstock with slightly wavy lines along each long side. Stamp *Leaf Whimsey* with green ink on the cream cardstock and heat set (see page 9). Stamp it again with silver ink on the black cardstock, sprinkle silver embossing powder on top of the wet ink and heat set.

**2** Place the cream cardstock on a cutting surface and use the knife to cut three wavy lines ½" wide, cutting ¼" from the top and bottom edges. Place the black cardstock on the cutting surface and use the knife to cut six wavy lines ½" wide, cutting horizontally across the piece. Weave them together to form a checkerboard pattern.

**3** Brush a thin layer of burgundy paint onto the metal, heat set and let dry. Use sandpaper to scratch off the edges of the foil. Glue the checkerboard piece centered on the foil and set aside.

**4** Brush burgundy paint onto each of the ⅜" wide metal strips, heat set and let dry. Sand each piece. Roll one end of the metal piece, leaving ½" flat at the other end. Repeat with each metal piece and set aside.

**5** Stamp *Believe*, *Dream* and *Aspire to BE* on the metal vase with black ink as shown. Sprinkle black embossing powder on top of the wet ink and heat set; let dry.

**6** Glue three metal coils evenly spaced along each side of the checkerboard plaque, so one end is tucked behind as shown. Glue the metal piece to the vase front.

**7** Cut 3½"–4½" lengths of fiber and floss. Place the ¾" metal strip vertically, then place the fiber and floss in the center of the metal with ¼" extending beyond the left edge and roll each outer end of the metal strip inward to the center to secure the fiber and floss. Glue the coil to the vase as shown.

*rubber stamps:*
   *Nine Point Star*
   *Small Swirl*
*chalk inks:*
   *Spanish Sand*
   *Painted Desert*
*acrylic paints:*
   *burnt umber*
   *burgundy*
*6¼"x6" black journal*
*thin copper metal:*
   *one 5"x6⅛" rectangle*
   *two ¾"x1" rectangles*
   *two ¾"x7" strips*
*1½"x6⅛" rectangle of white*
   *mulberry paper*
*5¾"x6⅛" ivory cardstock*
*2 yards of metallic burgundy*
   *embroidery floss*
*four 3/16" gold eyelets, eyelet*
   *setting tools*
*foam sponge*
*fine grain sandpaper*
*bone folder*
*X-acto® knife, cutting surface*
*metal ruler*
*pencil with eraser*
*tacky craft glue*
*embossing heat tool*

**1** Randomly stamp (see page 8) *Small Swirl* and *Nine Point Star* in red ink onto the 5"x6⅛" metal rectangle; heat set (see page 9).

**2** Burnish each stamped imprint into the metal. Sponge (see page 7) burnt umber and burgundy paints onto the metal; let dry. Sand the raised areas of the metal, allowing the paint to remain in the recessed areas. Cut out a 1⅝" square window centered near the top of the metal rectangle.

**3** Randomly stamp *Small Swirl* onto the cardstock with tan ink along the left edge. Place the embossed metal on top of it with the right sides even and lightly trace the window onto the cardstock, then remove the metal. Stamp *Nine Point Star* with tan ink within the traced area on the cardstock and heat set. Erase any visible pencil lines.

**4** Tear along the long left edge of the handmade paper. Align the metal on top of the cardstock with the right edges even, then slip the handmade paper strip between them with the torn edge extending ¼" beyond the metal left edge. Attach an eyelet (see page 6) in each corner of the metal to secure the pieces together.

**5** Wrap each ¾"x1" metal strip evenly spaced onto the left edge of the cardstock, with ¼" of each strip wrapping to the back.

**6** Randomly stamp *Small Swirl* with red ink onto portions of each ¾"x7" metal strip. Use the bone folder to press each stamped imprint into the metal. Sponge burgundy paint onto the metal; let dry. Sand the raised areas of the metal in a crisscross pattern, allowing the paint to remain in the recessed areas.

**7** Remove the wire binding from the journal (see page 54 for removing wire). Thread cord through the binding holes, lacing it up like a shoe and knotting the ends at the bottom. Wrap one strip around the journal cover right edge, folding the ends on the inside. Wrap the remaining metal strip to the left edge of the cover, wrapping the ends to the inside. Glue the cardstock piece centered on the journal cover.

# Leaf Treasure Box

Square Leaf rubber stamp
gold metallic pigment ink
Spanish Sand chalk ink
4¼"x4¼"x3¼" unfinished wood box
   with hinged lid
three ⅝" wide unfinished wood knobs
acrylic paints:
   burgundy
   burnt umber
thin copper metal:
   one 3¾"x4" rectangle
   four ¾"x2¾" rectangles
   three ¾"x1½" triangles
black handmade paper:
   one 4½" square
   four 1¼"x2¾" strips
fine grain sandpaper
liquid acrylic all-purpose sealer
decoupage glue
natural twine
bone folder
foam sponge
½" wide paintbrush
stipple brush
kitchen towel or craft foam
clean soft cloth
E6000® glue or Ultimate Glue®
embossing heat tool

**1** Apply a coat of sealer (see page 5) onto the box and lid; let dry. Lightly sand the box and lid; wipe clean. Paint the box and lid burgundy; let dry. Randomly stamp (see page 8) *Square Leaf* with gold ink over the surface of the box and heat set (see page 9). Apply a coat of sealer over the entire surface and let dry.

**2** Stamp *Square Leaf* onto the 3¾"x4" metal with red ink and heat set. Place the metal piece on a towel or craft foam and use the bone folder to press along the stamped image to create an embossed effect. Turn the piece over so the embossed side is face up. Sponge (see page 7) burgundy and burnt umber paint over the metal surface; let dry. Lightly sand the raised areas, leaving the paint in the recessed areas.

**3** Apply decoupage glue to the back of the 4½" black paper square, turn it on point and center on the lid, wrapping the corners onto the sides; let dry. Apply decoupage glue over the top and let dry. Glue the embossed metal piece centered on the black paper with the corners folded onto the sides as shown. Stipple gold ink onto the metal and heat set.

**4** Apply decoupage glue to the back of one black paper strip, then press it vertically onto a box corner, wrapping the ends to the inside top and bottom. Repeat for each box corner. Apply decoupage glue over each strip and let dry. Stamp *Square Leaf* onto each ¾"x2¾" metal strip with red ink and heat set. Place each strip on the towel or craft foam and use the bone folder to press along the stamped images. Sponge burgundy and burnt umber paint over the metal surface; let dry. Lightly sand, leaving the paint scratched. Glue one strip centered on each box corner.

**5** Paint the three metal triangles burgundy, let dry, then sand. Cut three 3" lengths of twine. Make a loop with each and glue the ends together. Lay the ends of one loop onto one end of the back of a metal triangle and roll the wide end of the triangle around the thin end of the paintbrush handle, beginning at the end with the twine. Repeat for the two remaining triangles. Glue one rolled foil piece to the left and right sides and the front of the lid with the twine loop hanging down as shown.

**6** Paint each knob burgundy and let dry. Sponge each knob with gold ink and let dry. Apply a coat of sealer to each knob and let dry. Glue knobs onto the box sides so the twine loop can be secured around them.

# Dreams are... Frame

*rubber stamps:*
  *Dreams*
  *Captain's Walk (ironwork border)*
*pigment inks:*
  *black*
  *gold*
  *copper*
*embossing powders:*
  *black*
  *copper*
  *gold*
*5"x7" matboard frame with a 3¹/₂"x5" opening*
*thin copper metal:*
  *1⁵/₈"x2³/₈" rectangle*
  *1³/₄" square*
*2¹/₂"x2" rectangle of cream suede paper*
*5¹/₈"x7¹/₈" rectangle of black cardstock*
*6" of 1¹/₂" wide wire mesh ribbon*
*fine grain sandpaper*
*foam adhesive tape*
*clear adhesive tape*
*foam sponge*
*¹/₄" wide flat paintbrush*
*low temperature glue gun, glue sticks*
*embossing heat tool*

**1** Sponge (see page 7) a section of the frame with gold ink, sprinkle gold embossing powder on top of the wet ink and heat set (see page 9). Repeat to cover the entire frame, then repeat the process twice with copper embossing powder to achieve a layered effect, allowing some of the gold to show through; let dry.

**2** Stamp *Captain's Walk* three to four times onto the cardstock center area with copper ink, sprinkle copper embossing powder on top and heat set.

**3** Lightly sand the metal rectangle lengthwise. Stamp *Dreams* onto the foil center with black ink, sprinkle black embossing powder on top and heat set. With the metal square turned on point, place the embossed rectangle centered on top and wrap the top and bottom points over the embossed rectangle. Glue the pieces centered on the suede paper.

**4** Cut fourteen 1" lengths of foam tape. Layer two to make double thick pieces. Place a double-thick piece onto the frame back at each outer corner, one at the right and one at the left side.

**5** Tape the wire mesh ends to the back of the frame, centered vertically in the window. Attach the frame centered on the black cardstock piece. Glue the stamped metal/suede paper piece onto the mesh ribbon center. Tuck the remaining double-thick foam tape layer centered under the mesh ribbon and metal piece.

# Polymer Clay

good
friends
are
forever

Polymer clay allows your rubber stamping to take on an intaglio effect—where the image sinks into the surface. By baking the clay, the permanent, carved-like image can be used in a number of ways. Check out some in this section!

# Tic Tac Toe Game Board Box

Tic Tac Toe rubber stamps (set of 3)
silver metallic pigment ink
silver embossing powder
acrylic paints:
  blue
  red
2¹⁄₈" square papier mâché box with lid
1³⁄₄" square of thin silver metal
4" square of metallic silver cardstock
³⁄₄" wide gray polymer clay
X-acto® knife, cutting surface
bone folder
brayer or rolling pin
foam pad or computer mouse pad
foam sponges
liquid acrylic all-purpose sealer
#1 liner paintbrush
tacky craft glue
embossing heat tool

**1** Remove the lid from the box. Apply a coat of sealer (see page 5) to the box and lid; let dry. Sponge (see page 7) blue paint over the entire box and lid; let dry. Randomly sponge (see page 8) silver ink onto the box and lid; heat set (see page 9). Apply sealer to the box and lid; let dry. Replace the lid on the box.

**2** Stamp *Tic Tac Toe* four times onto the silver cardstock with silver ink. While the ink is still wet, sprinkle silver embossing powder on top and heat set. Cut out each piece into a 1½" square and glue one to each side of the box.

**3** Stamp *Tic Tac Toe* onto the metal with silver ink and heat set. Place the silver metal square on the foam pad. Use the bone

folder to press along the stamped grid pattern into the foil. Turn the foil piece over so the raised grid is face up and glue it centered on the lid.

**4** Roll a 1½" square of polymer clay, ⅛" thick. Stamp four *X's* and four *O's* onto the clay square. Use the knife to cut out each letter into a ½" square. Follow the manufacturer's instructions to bake the clay and let cool completely.

**5** Sponge silver ink onto each letter tile and heat set. Use the brush to paint the indentations of the *X's* blue and the *O's* red and heat set. Glue six tiles onto the foil grid on the lid top and one of each remaining onto opposite sides of the box grids.

# Friendship Planters

rubber stamps:
  I'm So Glad
  Good Friends Forever
  Zebra Butterfly
  Gossamer Wings
pigment inks:
  Pastel Paintbox™
  metallic gold
  metallic silver
embossing powders:
  metallic gold
  metallic copper
silver acrylic paint
decorative chalks:
  pink
  green
  blue
  yellow
Paper Pizazz® Metallic Gold
  paper
white cardstock
white mulberry paper
two 2⅜"x2¼" terra cotta pots
polymer clay:
  1" wide ball of blue stone-look
  1" wide ball of pink stone-look
½ cup of rose potpourri
foam sponges
1" wide foam brush
liquid acrylic all-purpose sealer
2 craft sticks
two 2½"x2½"x2" blocks of floral
  foam
X-acto® knife, cutting surface
serrated knife
E6000® glue or Ultimate Glue®
clear adhesive tape
deckle pattern-edge scissors
embossing heat tool

**1** Use the foam brush to apply sealer (see page 5) to the inside and outside of each pot; let dry. Sponge (see page 7) pink or lavender ink onto each pot side, beginning lightly along the bottom and thicker along the rim. While the ink is still wet, sprinkle gold and copper embossing powders randomly onto each rim and heat set (see page 9).

**2** Insert a floral foam block into each pot, trimming with the knife if necessary and glue in place. Insert a craft stick into the center of each pot.

**3** Stamp I'm So Glad and Good Friends Forever onto white cardstock with gold ink. While the ink is still wet, sprinkle copper embossing powder onto each and heat set. Cut out each into a 3"x1⅞"

rectangle with the deckle scissors. Apply chalks with your fingertip around the edge of each rectangle in a rainbow fashion. Glue each onto gold paper and trim leaving a ⅛" border. Glue each piece on mulberry paper, tearing the edge to create a ¼" border. Glue one piece to the top of each craft stick. Cover the foam in each pot with potpourri and glue in place.

**4** Roll a 2¼"x2¼" rectangle of each polymer clay color, ⅛" thick. Stamp Zebra Butterfly twice onto the pink clay and Gossamer Wings twice onto the blue clay with silver ink. Use the X-acto® knife to cut out each stamped shape. Follow the manufacturer's instructions to bake the clay and allow to cool completely.

**5** Lightly sponge silver paint onto the front and sides of each clay piece and let dry. Glue one of each to the pots as shown and use tape to hold the pieces in place until the glue is completely dry.

# Stone Gecko Ceramic Pot

Gecko rubber stamp
Espresso chalk ink
metallic acrylic paints:
  gold
  silver
  copper
1¼" wide ball of beige polymer
  clay
5¼"x4⅝" white ceramic glazed
  flowerpot
1" wide foam brush
¼" wide flat paintbrush
18"x1" strip of natural burlap
  with frayed edges
brayer or rolling pin
3 strands of 16" long natural
  raffia
E6000® glue or Ultimate Glue®

**1** Roll the polymer clay to an 3"x2¼" oval, ⅛" thick. Stamp *Gecko* onto the clay (see page 11) with brown ink. Turn the pot on its side and gently press the clay onto the pot as shown. Follow the manufacturer's instructions to bake the clay and pot together so the clay will retain its curved shape; allow both pieces to cool thoroughly before removing the clay from the pot.

**2** Lightly paint the stamped *Gecko* imprint copper, then lightly brush the clay with metallic paints to create the look of stone; let dry. Glue the clay to the pot side.

**3** Wrap the burlap strip around the pot rim and glue in place. Hold the raffia strands together and tie them into a shoestring bow (see page 13) with 2" loops and 3" tails. Glue the bow knot to the burlap strip above the clay piece.

# Ancient Text Card

**rubber stamps:**
- Fleur de Lis
- Ancient Text
- Baroque Vine
- Captain's Walk
  - (ironwork border)

**chalk inks:**
- Espresso
- Spanish Sand
- Painted Desert

**pigment inks:**
- copper
- black

copper embossing powder

**acrylic paints:**
- brown
- burgundy

1" wide ball of terra cotta polymer clay

5⅛"x7" blank glossy card

- 2⅝"x5¼" ivory tag
- 2½"x7" natural corrugated cardboard
- thin copper metal
- three ³⁄₁₆" gold eyelets, eyelet setting tools
- 10" of 1½" wide ivory fiber mesh ribbon
- three ¾" wide decorative gold antique buttons
- 22" of natural twine
- foam sponge
- stipple brush
- #1 paintbrush
- fine grain sandpaper
- toothpick
- glue stick
- tacky craft glue
- tracing, transfer paper
- embossing heat tool

**1** Sponge (see page 7) tan, brown and red inks onto the entire card front; let dry. Stamp *Captain's Walk*, *Fleur de Lis* and *Ancient Text* onto the card front in random patterns with black ink; heat set (see page 9). Lightly sand the card front.

**2** Cut the cardboard, with a slightly irregular right edge to measure 2¼" wide on top and 2½" at the bottom. Randomly sponge (see page 8) the corrugated piece with copper ink. Sprinkle copper embossing powder on top of the wet ink and heat set. Open the card face up, place the corrugated piece on top with the left edge even with the card fold then attach an eyelet (see page 6) near the upper and lower left corners. Cut a 7" length of the mesh ribbon. Tuck the left edge of the mesh under the corrugated piece as shown and glue in place.

**3** Trace and transfer the triangle pattern (see page 13) to cut six copper metal triangles. Paint each metal strip with burgundy and brown paint; let dry. Sand each strip. Roll each strip around the paintbrush handle beginning at the wide end to form tube beads.

**4** Cut a 16" length of twine. Thread one end of the twine through the top eyelet, pull it onto the front, then thread on a metal bead, a button, another bead and repeat using all the beads and buttons. Thread the twine end into

the bottom eyelet, pull the twine ends together onto the outside center of the card fold and knot twice to secure. Trim each twine end to ½".

**5** Repeatedly stamp *Ancient Text* onto the tag with tan and brown inks; heat set. Tear the bottom of the tag off to form a 3½" long tag. Sponge the edges with copper ink, sprinkle copper embossing powder on top of the wet ink and heat set. Glue the remaining mesh ribbon to the bottom left corner of the tag, extending out ¼".

**6** Turn the tag so the hole is at the bottom. Glue the tag to the card front as shown. Open the card face up and attach an eyelet into the card front through the tag hole. Cut a 6" length of twine, then thread it through the tag eyelet, wrap it around the card edge and knot twice to secure.

**7** Roll a 1½" wide circle of polymer clay, ¼" thick. Stamp *Fleur de Lis* onto the clay with brown ink. Use the toothpick to draw a circle ⅛" from the clay edge, then draw a zigzag pattern along the outside of the circle. Follow the manufacturer's instructions to bake the clay and let cool completely. Use the small paintbrush to paint the *Fleur de Lis* shape with metallic copper ink and heat set. Glue the clay piece to the card front as shown.

Large Sun rubber stamp
Chianti pigment ink
acrylic paints:
    metallic silver
    metallic copper
paper clay
metallic embroidery floss:
    copper
    burgundy
two ½" wide burgundy glass beads
4" wide plastic disposable bowl
liquid acrylic all-purpose sealer
toothpick
spray water bottle
brayer or rolling pin
wax paper
E6000® glue or Ultimate Glue®

**1** Roll a 3" ball of paper clay then place it onto a sheet of wax paper. Flatten it halfway with your hand, then roll it out to a ⅛" thick, 8" wide circle. Lightly spray the clay with water to keep it moist. Smooth out any cracks in the clay.

**2** Stamp *Large Sun* gently onto the clay circle center with Chianti ink. Carefully lift the clay circle off the wax paper and place it into the plastic bowl, allowing the edges of the clay to fold inward naturally. Use the toothpick to poke ⅛" wide holes ¼" from the top edge and ½"-1" apart around the top edge.

**3** For the paper clay bead: Roll a 1" long, ½" wide log of clay, then cut off ⅛" from each end to form a tube shape. Insert the toothpick into the side of the tube and push it through to form a hole.

Ink *Large Sun* with Chianti ink and gently roll the clay bead along the stamp, then place the bead on one end. Let the bowl and bead dry overnight.

**4** Paint the bead and bowl with the metallic paints, using silver to highlight the sun beams and the bead and copper around the bowl rim; let dry. Apply sealer to the inside and outside of the bowl and let dry.

**5** Cut 30" lengths of the floss. Hold the floss together and thread them through the holes on the bowl, beginning at the bottom right. Insert the burgundy beads onto the floss in the lower left dish alcove and the paper bead in the lower right alcove. Pull the ends through the bottom right hole and trim the ends to 3". Glue the paper bead to the bowl side to secure.

# Glass Sea Life Bottle

rubber stamps:
  Angel Fish
  Three Fish
Pinwheel Petalpoint™
  pigment ink
3½"x1½"x4½" green-
  tinted glass oval
  bottle with cork
  stopper
ivory polymer clay
6mm pony beads: 4 teal,
  4 blue, 1 white
ten gold seed beads

green glass painted
  beads: one 10mm,
  one 8mm
24-gauge wire:
  blue
  gold
teal iridescent paint
¼" wide flat paintbrush
round toothpick
X-acto® knife, cutting
  surface
Glue Dots™

**1** Roll the clay into a 1" wide ball, then flatten it to ⅜" thick. Ink the *Three Fish* with assorted petals of the ink and press it twice into the polymer clay to make four fish images. Use the knife to cut around each imprint and smooth the edges. Insert a 2" length of the wire through one side and pull it out through the other side to create a bead. Repeat for three more fish.

**2** Roll a 1¾" clay ball and flatten it into a ⅜" thick oval. Ink the *Angel Fish* with assorted petals of the ink and press it into the clay. Use the toothpick to make a hole in the top of the clay oval, then poke it lightly around the edges to create texture. Bake all the clay pieces following the manufacturer's instructions; let cool.

**3** Paint around the fish on each bead and let dry. Cut the wire into four 20" lengths of gold and two 20" lengths of blue. Insert one end of the gold wire through a blue pony bead, wrap the wire around it three–four times, then insert the other end through a small fish bead and repeat with a teal bead at the other end. Allow a ½" space then repeat the process with a blue bead, fish and teal bead. Continue the process two more times using additional lengths of gold wire to form a circle.

**4** Insert a blue wire into the blue bead on the left side and wrap it around the bead four times. Coil the wire end around the end of the paintbrush handle. Remove the paintbrush and thread four seed beads onto the wire and wrap the end around the teal bead once. Repeat the process for the right side beads.

**5** Wrap the center of a gold wire length around the hole in the *Angel Fish* bead, then insert both ends through the large green bead, leave a ½" space then insert both ends through the white bead and wrap one wire end around each side of the bottle neck, twisting the ends in the back. Use Glue Dots™ to secure the back of the *Angel Fish* oval to the bottle. Place the beaded circle on the glass front with the top fish bead between the green and white beads. Use Glue Dots™ to hold it in place. Use one gold wire length to thread pony beads at each side of the top fish bead. Hold both wire ends together, thread through the white bead, then wrap the ends around the bottle neck and twist in the back.

**6** Wrap a blue wire around the bottle neck with the ends in front. Insert both ends into the small green bead, then insert a seed bead onto each end and coil each end seperately on the paintbrush handle. Remove the paintbrush. Wrap two blue wire lengths around the bottle neck, twisting the ends at the back to secure. Wrap a blue wire length from the front to the bottle neck back, then pull the ends to the opposite side and coil each end on the paintbrush handle.

# Shrink Plastic

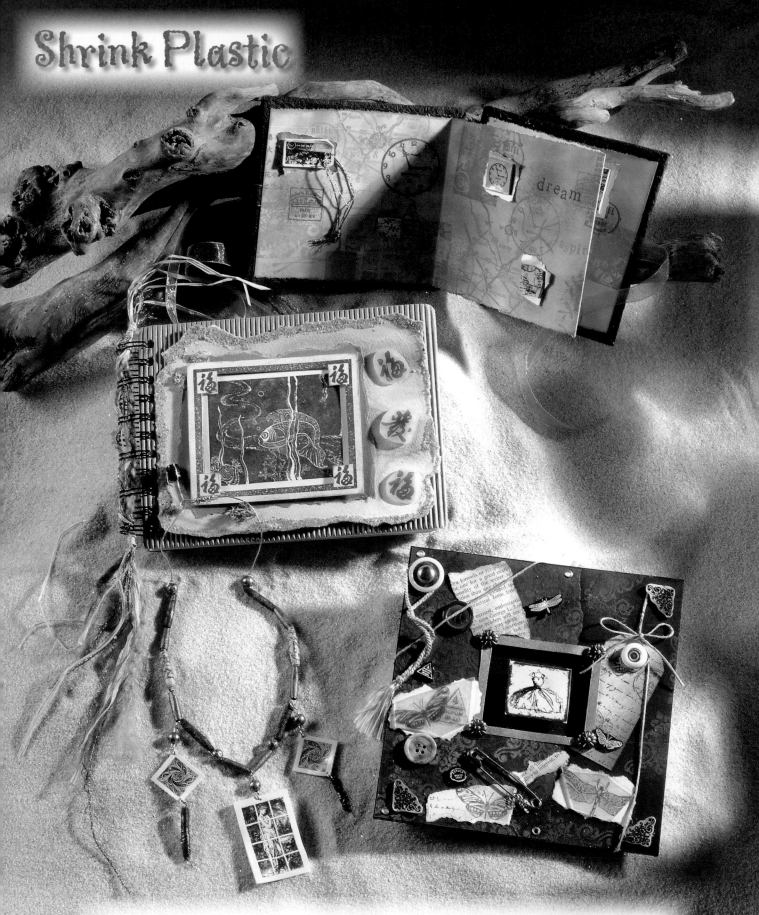

S hrink plastic is a fun way to show off your rubber stamping creativity. Stamp your image with one or multiple colors, cut out the piece and bake it according to the manufacturer's instructions. The miniature size is perfect for jewelry, frames and journals.

# Renaissance Necklace

rubber stamps:
  Renaissance
    Mosaic
  Framed Swirl
  Ancient Text
chalk inks:
  Painted Desert
  Espresso
gold pigment ink
ivory shrink plastic
mulberry papers:
  burgundy
  beige
  gold
beads:
  seven 5mm brass
  one 6mm burgundy
    glass
  2 gold seed

eight 5mm gold
  jump rings
metallic gold cord
24-gauge wire:
  gold
  silver
deckle pattern-edge
  scissors
1/8" hole punch
plastic coffee stir
  straw
decoupage glue
X-acto® knife,
  cutting surface
needle nose pliers
embossing heat tool

closeup of necklace

**1** Stamp *Renaissance Mosaic* onto shrink plastic (see page 12) using a combination of brown and red inks. Cut around the image, leaving a ¼" border and punch a hole centered at the top. Stamp *Framed Swirl* onto shrink plastic twice using red ink. Trim around each imprint with the deckle scissors, leaving a ¼" border. Turn each on point and punch a hole into the top and bottom corners. Follow the manufacturer's instructions to bake all the pieces; let cool.

**2** Cut six burgundy, two beige and six gold 1"x5" strips of paper. Stamp *Ancient Text* with brown ink onto the beige strips and heat set (see page 9). Stamp *Ancient Text* with gold ink onto the burgundy strips and heat set.

**3** Cut a 1" length from the straw. Place the embossed sides of the paper strips face down and wrap a ½" of one end of a strip onto a straw. Apply decoupage glue onto the back and continue to roll tightly around the straw. Apply decoupage glue to the entire paper surface. Remove the straw and set the paper bead aside to dry. Repeat for 13 more paper beads.

**4** Open and insert a jump ring (see page 13) into each shrink plastic hole, leaving the rings open. Cut three ¾" lengths of silver wire. Thread a brass bead onto one length with equal lengths of wire on each end. Use the pliers to bend each end into a loop. Repeat for two more beads. Insert the wire loop onto a jump ring at the top of each shrink plastic piece, then close the ring with the pliers.

**5** Cut two 4" lengths of gold wire. Insert one length through a burgundy paper bead with ¼" extending from the top. Bend the top wire section into a loop. Thread a seed bead onto the bottom wire end, then wrap it around the bead. Repeat for the other paper bead. Attach one to the bottom jump ring on each small shrink plastic piece. Close the jump rings.

**6** Cut a 24" length of gold cord. Thread a jump ring then the large shrink plastic piece onto the cord. Knot the center onto the jump ring. Thread a gold paper bead, brass bead and burgundy paper bead onto each cord end; then knot the cord onto the jump ring on the top of each small shrink plastic piece. Thread gold, beige, gold and burgundy paper beads onto each end, then a brass bead and knot the cord on each side to secure the beads in place.

**7** Tie the burgundy bead onto the cord left end of the necklace. Fold 3" of the cord right end then wrap the end around itself to form a wrapped loop. Cover the wrapped loop with decoupage glue to secure it. To clasp, thread the bead through the loop.

# Heirloom Dress Collage Frame

**rubber stamps:**
  Filigree Corner
  Lettre
  My Mother's Dress
  Far Off Posts (set of 4)
  Gossamer Wings
  Zebra Butterfly
**chalk inks:**
  Painted Desert
  Espresso
**pigment inks:**
  copper
  frosted white
  black picture perfect
**copper embossing**
  **powder**
**shrink plastic:**
  brown
  beige
  clear
**cardstock:**
  3" square of ivory
  gold

5"x7" burgundy paper
black matboard:
  7" square
  6"x5½" rectangle
  1⅝"x3¼" ivory tag
natural twine
five 5mm gold jump
  rings
four ³⁄₁₆" gold eyelets,
  eyelet setting tools
book page
6" long gold cord with
  tassel
buttons:
  four ½" wide gold
    daisies
  four ⅝"-1" wide
    assorted
2¼" gold safety pin
X-acto® knife, cutting
  surface
tacky craft glue
stipple brush
foam adhesive tape
wire cutters

**1** Randomly stamp (see page 8) *Filigree Corner* in red and copper inks onto the square matboard and burgundy rectangle; heat set (see page 9). Tear along the long right edge of the burgundy piece then place it on the black matboard with the left edges even. Attach an eyelet (see page 6) in each corner of the burgundy piece to secure it to the matboard.

**2** Stamp the tag with *Lettre*, then portions of the remaining stamps with brown ink. Stipple (see page 7) the edges with brown ink and heat set. Glue the tag to the matting as shown. Place the matting on a cutting surface and use the knife to cut out a 2½"x2" window in the center to form a frame. Cut two ¼"x3" and two ¼"x2¼" strips of gold cardstock then glue them to the window edges.

**3** Cut the shanks off the back of each button. Glue a daisy button to each window corner and a large button to the tag top. Stamp *My Mother's Dress* onto beige shrink plastic with black ink. Stamp *Zebra Butterfly, Gossamer Wings* and two of the *Far Off Posts* onto brown shrink plastic with white ink. Stamp *Filigree Corner* three times onto beige shrink plastic with red ink. Cut around the image shapes. Follow the manufacturer's instructions to bake the shrink plastic; let cool.

**4** Cut two irregular 6"x3" shapes from the clear shrink plastic. Follow the manufacturer's instructions to bake the blank shrink plastic pieces;

74

let cool. Stamp *Zebra Butterfly* and one of the *Far Off Posts* onto one piece and *Gossamer Wings* onto the other, all in brown ink; heat set.

**5** Tear three irregular shapes from ivory cardstock. Stamp *Zebra Butterfly* and part of *Lettre* onto one with brown ink. Tear 1½"x2½" and 1½"x½" pieces from a book. Stipple each cardstock and book piece with brown ink. Heat set each piece.

**6** Glue the stamped cardstock piece near the lower left corner of the frame. Glue each clear shrink plastic piece to a stippled cardstock piece, then glue each to the frame as shown. Cut a 24" length of twine, wrap it around the right side of the frame and tie the ends into a shoestring bow (see page 13) above the tag top as shown. Cut a 16" twine length and wrap it around the upper left corner, knotting the ends at the back. Place the jump rings on the safety pin and glue to the frame as shown. Glue a plastic *Filigree Corner* to each lower and upper right corner. Glue a large button to the upper left corner, then hang the tassel onto the button and glue to secure.

**7** Use foam tape to attach the remaining matboard piece to the back of the frame. Sponge the edges of *My Mother's Dress* with copper ink, sprinkle embossing powder on top and heat set. Attach the piece centered in the frame window with foam tape. Decorate the frame with the remaining items.

# Accordian Travel Journal

**rubber stamps:**
- Tomorrow's Territory
- On the Metro Wall
- Lettre
- Antique Compass
- Passporte
- Far Off Posts
- Aspire to Be
- Dream
- Leaf Whimsy
- London Calling
- Love Letters
- NYC Tag Art
- Asian Wrapper

**chalk inks:**
- Spanish Sand
- Lavender Flower
- Pacific Horizon

**pigment inks:**
- Pink Porcelain
- gold metallic
- ivory shrink plastic
- 20"x5" white cardstock
- Paper Pizazz® Metallic Gold paper
- 12"x12" burgundy handmade paper
- two 5½"x5⅜" rectangles of matboard
- deckle pattern-edge scissors
- 30" of ⅝" wide gold sheer ribbon

**metallic embroidery floss:**
- gold
- lavender
- ⅛" hole punch
- stipple brush
- foam sponge
- tacky craft glue
- bone folder
- embossing heat tool

**1** Trim along the top and bottom edges of the cardstock with the deckle scissors. Use the bone folder to score it every 5" to form three accordian folds. Sponge (see page 7) tan and pink inks over the entire cardstock; let dry.

**2** Randomly stamp (see page 8) each stamp onto the cardstock piece using all the inks, overlapping images, repeating images with different colors and allowing some images to extend off the paper; let dry. Ink along the cardstock edge with gold ink, then heat set (see page 9).

**3** Stamp a variety of images onto shrink plastic with lavender ink to make eight pieces. Cut out each piece to a 2"x3" rectangle, then punch a hole near the top of two pieces. Follow the manufacturer's instructions for baking the shrink plastic.

**4** Cut two 7" lengths of each floss color. Thread one of each color through the holes in the two pieces, pull the ends even and knot. Tear gold paper to glue under each plastic piece and glue in place.

**5** Glue the matted plastic pieces onto the stamped journal pages so two pieces are on each scored section. Cut the ribbon in half. Glue 2" of one ribbon end centered at the back of each short side of the stamped cardstock so the other end extends out; then trim each exposed end at an angle.

**6** Cut two 6½"x6⅜" and two 5⅛"x5" rectangles of burgundy paper. Cover each matboard rectangle with a large burgundy piece, wrapping the long edges onto the back side, then the short edges onto the back and gluing to secure. Glue a smaller burgundy rectangle centered on the back side.

**7** With the back side of a covered matboard facing up, glue the left page of the journal centered on it, then glue the right page centered on the back side of the remaining cover piece. Fold the pieces together then tie the ribbons together to secure.

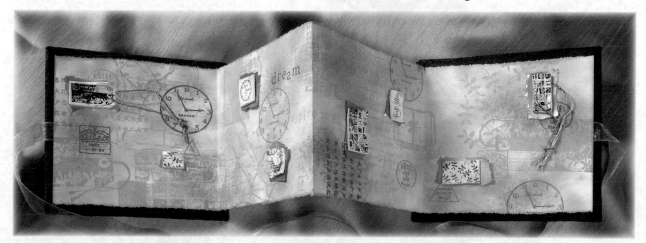

rubber stamps:
   *Heirloom Quilt*
   *Rose*
chalk inks:
   Espresso
   Painted Desert
   Brushed Sage
pigment inks:
   gold
   cream white
shrink plastic:
   brown
   white
gold embossing powder
6"x12" rectangle of white burlap
5¾" square of dark red handmade
   paper
12" square of ivory textured
   cardstock
metallic gold cord
buttons:
   four ½" wide ivory
   one ¾" wide purple
2" square of polyester fiberfill
stipple brush
sewing needle
X-acto® knife, cutting surface
long-handled craft tweezers
low temperature glue gun, glue sticks
embossing heat tool

**1** Stamp *Heirloom Quilt* four times onto white shrink plastic with brown and red inks. Cut out each piece, leaving a ½" border. Stipple (see page 7) each piece with brown and red inks.

**2** Stamp *Rose* twice onto white shrink plastic with red on the blossom and green on the leaves. Stipple the corners of each piece with red ink. Clean the stamp, then restamp *Rose* twice onto brown shrink plastic with white ink. Cut each out into a square. Stipple the corners of each piece with white ink.

**3** Follow the manufacturer's instructions to bake all the shrink plastic pieces; let cool. Use the tweezers to hold the center of each piece, brush the edges with gold ink, sprinkle gold embossing powder on top of the wet ink and heat set (see page 9).

**4** Cut a 4" square and a 6"x7" rectangle of burlap and fray the edges of each. Center the burlap

square onto the red paper square. Thread the needle with gold cord and sew three sides of the burlap onto the paper. Insert the fiberfill into the opening, then sew the fourth side, knotting the cord end at the back.

**5** Sew the purple button onto the center of the burlap, knotting the ends at the back. Sew an ivory button centered on the inside edge of each side, knotting the ends at the back. Sew the top edge of the red paper centered on the large burlap piece, knotting the ends at the back. Glue the other sides of the paper to the burlap. Glue a *Heirloom Quilt* piece near each corner, then glue the *Rose* pieces onto the center burlap piece as shown.

**6** Cut the cardstock to a 7"x12" rectangle, then fold it in half to form a 6"x7" card. Stipple the edges of the card front with red and let dry. Glue the burlap piece to the card front.

# Harmony Fish Journal

rubber stamps:
   Harmony Fish
   Harmony
   Prosperity
pigment inks:
   Royal Blue
   Cyan Blue
   Sky Blue
clear embossing powder
iridescent paints:
   blue
   purple
clear shrink plastic
8"x6" spiral-bound journal with
   corrugated cover
cardstock:
   5"x6" white
   5"x10" light blue
fibers:
   blue
   brown
metallic embroidery floss:
   blue
   copper
4 strands of natural raffia
1" square tuft of Spanish moss
1 tablespoons of sand
1/4" hole punch
tacky craft glue
Glue Dot™ Pop-Ups, Glue Dots™
X-acto® knife, cutting surface
1/2" wide flat paintbrush
embossing heat tool

**1** Tear a 7¼"x5½" rectangle of white cardstock. Lightly brush blue and purple iridescent paint onto the rectangle; let dry. Apply tacky glue along the edges, sprinkle sand on top and lightly dust away any excess; let dry. Use Glue Dots™ to adhere the rectangle centered on the journal cover.

**2** Use a variety of the pigment inks to stamp *Harmony Fish* twice onto white cardstock. Cut an ⅛" border around one imprint and a 3/16" border around the other. Place the larger imprint on a cutting surface and use the knife to cut out the frame with the corner characters. Center the frame over the small fish imprint with the corner characters aligned, then use Pop-Up Glue Dots™ to secure the pieces together at the corners.

**3** Tear a 5¼"x4¼" rectangle of blue cardstock, then glue the framed *Harmony Fish* centered on top. Glue it to the journal cover 1¾" from the right edge. Glue tufts of moss to the upper left and lower edge of the *Harmony Fish* mat.

**4** Stamp *Harmony* twice and *Prosperity* once onto shrink plastic with royal blue ink. Cut an oval shape around each character. Follow the manufacturer's instructions to bake the shrink plastic pieces. Once cooled, use Glue Dots™ to attach the plastic pieces to the journal cover as shown.

**5** Cut 15"–23" lengths of the fibers, floss and raffia. Hold the lengths together, weave them through the spiral binding on the journal, then knot the strands together above and below the spirals.

# Plastic

R ecycle that unwanted CD into an artform all its own! Sand off any film on each side of the CD, apply a coat of sealer on top and stamp it with one or a combination of images. Cut it into random pieces to simulate broken glass. The results are fabulous.

# Freedom Mosaic Card

Freedom Collage rubber
   stamp
chalk inks:
   Blue Suede
   Brushed Sage
   Pacific Horizon
   Painted Desert
silver pigment ink
silver embossing powder
Paper Flair™ 5"x6½" blank
   card
Paper Pizazz® papers:
   6½"x5¼" Metallic Silver
   6½"x5" red
6"x4¾" white mulberry paper
2 blank compact disks
fine grain sandpaper
stipple brush
long-handled craft tweezers
E6000® glue or Ultimate
   Glue®
foam sponge
clean soft cloth
heavy-duty scissors
liquid acrylic all-purpose
   sealer
embossing heat tool

1 Sand both sides of each CD to remove the
   protective film and wipe off any dust with a
clean cloth. Apply a coat of sealer to each CD and
let dry. Stamp *Freedom Collage* onto one disk with
red, green and blue inks. (The middle of the image
will not get stamped because of the hole in the disk,
so re-ink the stamp and stamp the center portion
onto the second disk for a full image.) Heat set (see
page 9) each disk.

2 While the disks are still hot, cut out the images
   with a pair of heavy-duty scissors. (The heat
allows for easier cutting.)

3 Pick up one stamped disk piece in the center
   with the tweezers and sponge silver ink along

the edges. While the ink is still wet, sprinkle silver
embossing powder on top and heat set. Repeat for
each stamped disk piece.

4 Tear a 5½"x4¼" rectangle of mulberry paper
   and a 6"x4¾" rectangle of silver paper. Glue
the mulberry paper centered on the silver. Glue
the disk pieces in a circular mosaic pattern on the
mulberry paper.

5 Glue the red paper to the card front. Turn
   the card so the fold is at the top and glue the
mosaic piece centered on the card front.

## Preparing the CD:

To prepare a CD for stamping, sand each side to remove all
the protective film and coating. Apply a coat of sealer to
each side to prevent the ink from bleeding when an image is
stamped onto it. Note: some CD plastics will not appear clear
when sanded. This should not deter results from stamping.

79

# Message Tag

rubber stamps:
 Leaf Whimsey
 Lettre
chalk inks:
 Brushed Sage
 Pacific Horizon
 Evergreen
2⅝"x5¼" white tag
blank compact disk
1¾"x5¼" of white mulberry
 paper
⅜"x 3" of white cardstock
½"x3" of thin copper metal
four 3/16" wide gold eyelets,
 eyelet setting tools

two 10" strands of natural
 raffia
heavy-duty scissors
fine grain sandpaper
X-acto® knife, cutting surface
stipple brush
glue stick
liquid acrylic all-purpose
 sealer
E6000® glue or Ultimate Glue®
black pen
metal ruler
clean soft cloth
embossing heat tool

**1** Stipple (see page 7) green and blue inks onto the tag. Stamp *Lettre* repeatedly with green inks to cover the tag then heat set (see page 9). Glue the mulberry paper centered on the tag.

**2** Sand the compact disk to remove the protective film and wipe off any dust with a clean cloth. Stamp *Leaf Whimsey* onto one half of the disk and *Lettre* on the other half with green ink. Heat set the entire disk.

**3** While the disk is still hot use scissors to cut six ¾" wide irregular shapes of each half of the disk for a total of 12 pieces.

**4** Place the metal strip on a cutting surface and use the knife and ruler to cut a ¼"x1⅝" window in the center. Glue the white cardstock strip behind the metal, then attach an eyelet (see page 6) centered at the top and bottom to secure the pieces together. Use the pen to write "Love" on the cardstock.

**5** Attach an eyelet centered at the top and bottom of the tag. Place the metal strip centered on the tag, then thread raffia through the eyelets to secure it in place. Knot the raffia ends and trim to 1½". Glue six plastic pieces along each side of the tag.

### Where can I find a CD?

*A*lthough the CD's that arrive in the mail for marketing purposes are the most economical means for getting a CD for your project, there are many other sources. Try garage sales or thrift shops for a cheap alternative. Or purchase blank CD's from a computer or office supply store.

# Glass Imagery Bottle

Contemplation rubber
  stamp
Enchantment
  Petalpoint™ ink pads
Top Boss™ Embossing
  Ink
black permanent ink
clear embossing powder
2¼"x4¼" clear glass
  triangle bottle with
  cork stopper
gold micro beads
beads:
  ½" clear,
  ⅛" clear,
  1/16" gold

metallic embroidery
  floss:
  blue
  gold
  lavender
  black with multi-
    colored metallic
    flecks
blank CD disk
Terrifically Tacky Tape™
fine grain sandpaper
long-handled craft
  tweezers
heavy-duty scissors
E6000® glue or Ultimate
  Glue®
embossing heat tool

**1** Prepare the CD for stamping (see page 12). Stamp *Contemplation* onto the CD with black ink and allow to thoroughly dry.

**2** Warm the CD slightly with the embossing heat tool then cut out the stamped imprint. Cover the CD with embossing ink and heat set (see page 9). Repeat two-three more times to achieve a thick glass-like layer over the imprint.

**3** Turn the CD face down and ink the back with assorted petals of the pigment ink. Hold the CD with the tweezers, cover the back with clear embossing powder and heat set.

**4** Cover the top right and bottom right of the CD with tacky glue and pour micro beads on top; let dry. Glue the CD to the bottle front. Cover ¼" around the lower bottle neck with tacky tape and press micro beads onto it; let dry.

**5** Cut 20" lengths of each floss color. Hold them together and wrap them twice around the upper bottle neck and knot. Thread the large clear bead onto several floss strands, push it against the knot, wrap the remaining strands around the bead and secure it by wrapping Terrifically Tacky Tape™ around the strands just below the bead. Press micro beads onto the tape. Thread the remaining beads randomly on a floss strand and knot it below to secure it in place.

# Fabric

Take fabric painting to a unique level with rubber stamping. Here are ways to use leather, silk, muslin and velvet in ways you only imagined. Now, you can create your own fabulous fabrics!

We wish you a Merry Christmas AND A Happy New Year

# Leather Nature Journal

rubber stamps:
  Leaves & Acorns
  Oak Leaf
    Silhouette
chalk inks:
  Brushed Sage
  Espresso
gold pigment ink
Embossing Magic™

gold embossing
  powder
6"x8" leather-
  bound personal
  organizer
leather sealant
foam sponge
embossing heat tool

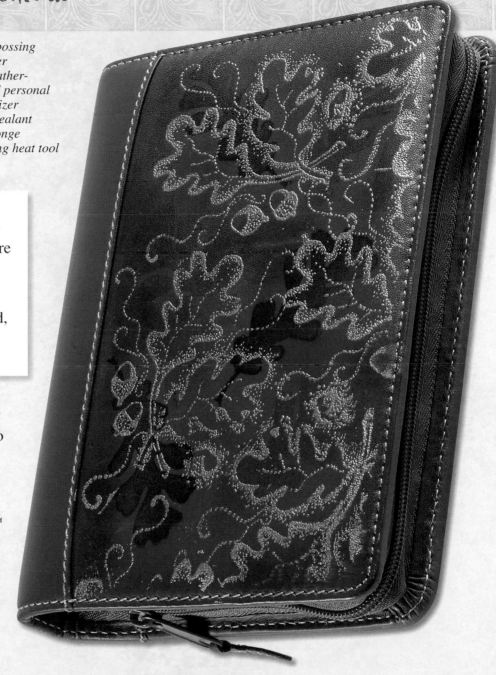

**B**efore you begin: Embossing Magic™ is a small pillow you rub onto the surface before stamping and embossing. It prevents embossing powder from adhering to the surface other than where you stamped, so your embossed images are perfect each time!

**1** Randomly stamp *Oak Leaf Silhouette* (see page 8) onto the organizer front cover with green and brown inks and heat set (see page 9).

**2** Wipe Embossing Magic™ over the front cover. Randomly stamp *Leaves & Acorns* onto the front with gold ink, sprinkle gold embossing powder on top of the wet ink and heat set.

**3** Lightly sponge brown ink (see page 7) around the front cover edges and heat set; let dry thoroughly. Apply a coat of leather sealant over the front cover (see page 11) and let dry. Repeat steps 1–3 for the back cover.

## Heat Setting Leather:

**T**ime for heat setting leather will vary (10–60 seconds) depending on the grade of the leather material. With all the leather-look vinyls and variations in leather, you may wish to first stamp and heat set a small section inside the journal to determine the best heat setting for your project.

# Leather Holiday Scrapbook Page

rubber stamps:
  Fancy Ornament
  Merry Christmas & Happy New
    Year
  Fern
chalk inks:
  Brushed Sage
  Pacific Horizon
gold pigment ink
Embossing Magic™
gold embossing powder
cardstock:
  12" square of ivory
  3⅞"x2⅝" rectangle of ivory
  7"x8" metallic gold textured
  9"x9½" rectangle of black leather
ribbon:
  30" of ⅝" wide sage green sheer
    with satin wire edges
  2⅓ yards of ⅛" wide kelly green
    satin
foam sponge
leather sealant
color copies of photographs:
  4"x3"
  3"x4"
Glue Dots™
embossing heat tool

**1** Randomly stamp *Fern* (see page 8) onto the outer edge of the cardstock square with green and blue inks to form a 2" wide border. Lightly sponge green ink (see page 7) onto the border and heat set (see page 9). Round the corners.

**2** Randomly stamp *Fern* onto the leather with green and blue inks; heat set. Wipe Embossing Magic™ (see page 6) over the leather surface. Stamp *Fancy Ornament* in the upper right corner with gold ink, sprinkle gold embossing powder on top of the wet ink and heat set. Apply a coat of leather sealant over the leather (see page 11) and let dry. Use Glue Dots™ to attach the leather piece to the cardstock, centered 2" from the top edge.

**3** Stamp *Merry Christmas & Happy New Year* onto the ivory rectangle with green ink. Sponge the edge with gold ink, sprinkle gold embossing powder on top of the wet ink and heat set.

*This scrapbook page is not acid-free, so use copies of your photos instead of the originals.*

**4** Cut one 4⅝"x3⅜" and two 4½"x3½" rectangles of gold cardstock. Cut six 6" lengths of the narrow ribbon. Wrap one length from side-to-side on each gold rectangle, gluing the ends at the back. Wrap another length from top to bottom, gluing the ends at the back. Glue the sentiment rectangle centered on the largest rectangle. Glue the photos to the remaining rectangles. Glue the pieces to the leather as shown.

**5** Cut three 5" lengths each of the ribbons. Tie a knot in the center of each sheer ribbon, then wrap the center of a narrow ribbon length around the sheer ribbon center and knot. Glue the ribbon pairs to the page as shown.

**6** Cut a 14" length of narrow ribbon. Wrap it around the page top, gluing the ends at the back. Use the remaining sheer ribbon to make a shoestring bow (see page 13) with 2" loops and 3" tails. Trim each tail at an angle. Wrap the remaining narrow ribbon around the bow center and knot. Glue the bow centered on the page top.

# Fern Scrapbook Album

rubber stamps:
  Filigree Corner
  Feather Fern
Evergreen chalk ink
gold pigment ink
gold acrylic paint
12" square spiral-
  bound scrapbook
10"x11" matboard
5"x7" metallic gold
  frame with a
  3"x4½" opening
12" square of light
  green silk fabric
1½"x2⅛" white
  scallop-top tag

ribbon:
  30" of 2⅛" wide
    white sheer
  4⅓ yards of ¼"
    wide ivory
    satin
iron, ironing board
1" wide foam brush
4"x6" photo
low temperature
  glue gun, glue
  sticks
embossing heat tool

**1** Remove the spiral from the scrapbook (see page 54) and set the pages and back cover aside. Paint a gold 2" wide border around the outer edge of the front cover; let dry. Apply a second coat of paint and let dry.

**2** Randomly stamp (see page 8) *Feather Fern* onto the silk with green ink. Stamp *Filigree Corner* 2" in from the upper left and lower right corners of the silk with gold ink. Let dry. Set the iron to permanent press (with no steam). Turn the fabric face down on the ironing board and iron the fabric for 1-2 minutes to heat set the ink; allow to cool.

**3** With the fabric face down, place the matboard in the center and wrap the fabric sides onto the matboard and glue; then wrap the top and bottom edges onto the matboard and glue to secure. Turn the fabric piece face up and glue it centered to the scrapbook cover.

**4** Glue the photo to the back of the gold frame so it shows through the window. Glue the frame centered 1¼" from the right edge of the silk.

**5** Cut the sheer ribbon into one 14" and two 8" lengths. Wrap the 14" length around the cover top and bottom overlapping the left side of the fabric piece; glue the ends at the back. Wrap an 8" length diagonally around the upper and lower right corners of the cover, gluing the ends at the back.

**6** Stamp *Filigree Corner* diagonally onto the tag with gold ink. Sponge (see page 7) the tag edges with gold ink and heat set (see page 9). Cut a 6" length of ivory ribbon, thread it through the tag hole and knot it to secure. Glue the tag to the corner as shown.

**7** Cut one 14", one 12" and two 8" lengths of the ¼" ribbon. Wrap the 14" length on the left side of the 14" sheer ribbon and glue the ends at the back. Wrap an 8" length around each corner as shown, gluing the ends at the back. Use the 12" ribbon length to make a shoestring bow (see page 13) with ¾" loops and 1½" tails, then glue it centered on the gold frame top.

**8** Place the cover on the pages and back, aligning the drill holes. With the remaining ribbon, begin at the bottom hole and thread the ribbon through, wrap it around the outer edge and back into the same hole, leaving a 6" tail. Thread the other end through the next hole, wrap it around the outer edge and into the third hole, lacing it through all the holes. Wrap it once more around the top hole, then pull it down to the bottom tail and tie the ends into a shoestring bow with ½" loops and 1" tails.

# Celestial Candlestick Lamp

Design Elements Collection
 rubber stamps
pigment inks:
 gold
 silver
embossing powders:
 gold
 silver
Embossing Magic™
6¾" tall battery-powered
 candlestick lamp with bulb
4" tall white candlestick
 lampshade

18"x7" rectangle of white
 muslin fabric
gold micro beads
¼" wide Terrifically Tacky
 Tape™
18"x7" rectangle of scrap
 paper
tacky craft glue
¼" wide flat paintbrush
embossing heat tool

*Before you begin:* Embossing Magic™ is a small pillow you rub onto the surface before stamping and embossing. It prevents embossing powder from adhering to the surface other than where you stamped, so your embossed images are perfect each time!

1 Wrap the scrap paper around the lampshade and trace the top and bottom edges onto the paper to make a pattern, marking where the two seams meet. Remove the paper, cut out the shape ½" larger on each edge. Place the paper pattern onto the fabric and cut out the shape.

2 Rub Embossing Magic™ over the entire fabric piece. Starting at one end, randomly stamp (see page 8) the *Swirl* and each *Star* from the *Design Elements Collection* onto the fabric with gold ink. While the ink is still wet, sprinkle gold embossing powder on top and heat set (see page 9), being careful not to over heat any area. Repeat using the same stamps with silver ink, apply silver embossing powder on top and heat set. Repeat until the fabric piece is covered, leaving about 1" between each stamped image.

3 Turn the fabric piece face down and apply glue to the top and bottom edges. Begin with the left end and wrap the fabric piece around the shade, pressing the top and bottom glued edges onto the inside. Fold the right raw end under ¼" to overlap the seams and glue in place.

4 Cut a 9½" and 16" length of Terrifically Tacky Tape™. Wrap the short length around the shade top and the longer around the shade bottom edge. Remove the backing and press micro beads onto the tape.

5 Apply glue onto the base of the lamp and press micro beads on top to cover the base; let dry. Place the lampshade on the lamp.

## Heat Setting Fabrics:

*Time for heat setting fabrics will vary (20-60 seconds) depending on your iron and the fabric. You may wish to practice on a scrap piece of fabric to determine the best combination of heat and time.*

# Embossed Velvet Asian Bag

rubber stamps:
  Prosperity
  Chinese Calligraphy (set of 3)
metallic gold fabric paint
6"x5¼" canvas gift bag with handles
3½"x4" burgundy velvet (rayon/silk
  mix is best)

10" length of 1" wide gold metal mesh
  ribbon
2¾"x3¼" matboard
1" wide foam brush
spray bottle with water
iron & ironing board
5¾"x5" piece of wax paper
tacky craft glue

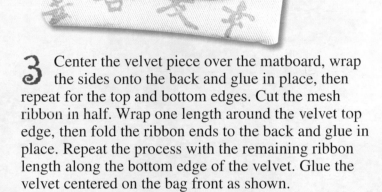

**1** Place wax paper inside the bag to protect against ink bleeding through the layers. Use the foam brush to apply gold paint to the raised area of one of the *Chinese Calligraphy* stamps. Press the stamp onto the bag front and gently pull straight up to remove. Repeat the procedure with the other stamps in the collection for a random pattern on the bag front, repeating stamps images to cover the front. Let dry, then repeat the process for the bag back.

**2** Preheat the iron to the wool or cotton setting with no steam. Place the *Prosperity* stamp face up on the ironing board. Spray the nap (fuzzy) side of the velvet with a mist of water, then center the nap side face down over the stamp. Place the iron on top of the velvet and stamp and keep as steady as possible for 10–30 seconds. Remove the iron and let the velvet cool before removing the stamp.

**3** Center the velvet piece over the matboard, wrap the sides onto the back and glue in place, then repeat for the top and bottom edges. Cut the mesh ribbon in half. Wrap one length around the velvet top edge, then fold the ribbon ends to the back and glue in place. Repeat the process with the remaining ribbon length along the bottom edge of the velvet. Glue the velvet centered on the bag front as shown.

# Embossed Velvet Box

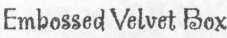

rubber stamps:
  Leaf Whimsey
  Design Elements Collection
Espresso chalk ink
gold pigment ink
metallic gold acrylic paint
3" square papier mâché box with lid
6" square of brown velvet (polyester
  blend)
four ⅝" unfinished wood plugs
½" wide gold button

metallic gold thread
3" square of cardboard
¼" wide flat paintbrush
spray bottle with water
iron & ironing board
wire cutters
low temperature glue gun, glue
  sticks
embossing heat tool

**1** Preheat the iron to the wool or cotton setting with no steam. Ink *Leaf Whimsey* with gold ink, then place it face up on the ironing board. Spray the nap (fuzzy) side of the velvet with a mist of water, then center the nap side face down over the stamp. Place the iron on top of the velvet and stamp and keep as steady as possible for 10–30 seconds until the image sets. Let cool. Repeat the process to cover the velvet.

**2** Place the velvet face down, then place the lid centered face down on the velvet square. Wrap the velvet edges onto the lid inside and glue in place. Sponge (see page 7) gold paint onto the cardboard square and let dry. Glue the cardboard to the lid inside.

**3** Stamp three rows of the *Figure 8 Border* from the *Design Elements Collection* on each side of the box with brown ink; heat set (see page 9). Paint each plug gold; let dry. Glue a plug to each bottom corner. Place the lid on the box. Cut two 15" lengths of thread, wrap them around the lid sides and knot in front. Trim the tails to 1". Cut the shank from the button, then glue it to the thread knot.

# Craft Foam

# Craft Foam Icon Card

rubber stamps:
  Carved Shell
  Carved Heart
  Carved Star
  Carved Flower
chalk inks:
  Pacific Horizon
  Blue Shadow
  Spanish Sand
  Espresso
metallic gold acrylic paint
craft foam:
  4"x7½" rectangle of turquoise
  4"x7" rectangle of tan
4½"x6" speckled cream notecard
silver wire mesh rectangles:
  4"x5½"
  4"x4½"
four ³⁄₁₆" wide silver eyelets
eyelet setting tools
Glue Dots™
foam sponge

1   Cut a 4"x5½" rectangle of turquoise foam. Place the [4]x5½" wire mesh over the foam. [U]se a sponge to lightly dab gold [p]aint onto the foam through the mesh, then remove the mesh. Brush gold paint along the foam [e]dges; let dry.

2   Open the card face up. Center the foam piece on the card front and attach an eyelet (see page 6) into each foam corner to secure it to the card. Cut a 3⅜"x3¾" rectangle of tan foam. Use Glue Dots™ to secure the tan foam piece centered on the turquoise foam piece. Center the 4"x4½" rectangle of wire mesh over the tan foam and secure it with Glue Dots™.

3   Cut a 2"x4" rectangle of turquoise foam. Sponge (see page 7) tan and Pacific Horizon inks randomly on the foam. Stamp *Carved Shell* and *Carved Flower* onto the foam piece with Blue Shadow ink; let dry. Cut out each stamped image, leaving an ⅛" border. Brush gold ink around the edges and lightly over each stamped image.

4   Cut a 2"x4" piece of tan foam. Sponge tan and Pacific Horizon inks randomly on the foam. Stamp *Carved Star* and *Carved Heart* onto the foam piece with brown ink; let dry. Cut out each stamped image, leaving an ⅛" border. Brush gold ink around the edges and lightly over each stamped image.

5   Attach Glue Dots™ to the back of each foam piece, then position them on the card front as shown.

## Stamping on Craft Foam:

**S**tamping on craft foam is a great way to jazz up this ordinary craft material, though drying time is longer than that of paper and other surfaces.

# Magnetic Foam Frame

*Happy Birthday Collection rubber
   stamps
blue suede chalk ink
silver acrylic paint
4½"x5½" rectangle of turquoise
   craft foam
4¼"x4¾" rectangle of ivory
   cardstock
five ³⁄₁₆" silver eyelets, eyelet
   setting tools
two ¾" wide circular magnets
ten 5mm silver jump rings
two ½" wide silver/white buttons
24-gauge silver wire
X-acto® knife, cutting surface
tacky craft glue
Glue Dots™
photograph
¼" wide flat paintbrush
⅛" hole punch
wire cutters*

**1** Randomly stamp the *Present, Cake, Stars,
Confetti* and *Happy Birthday* from the *Happy
Birthday Collection* onto the foam with blue ink;
let dry.

**2** Place the foam on a cutting surface and use
the knife to cut out a 2"x3½" window angled
to the right near the upper right corner. Brush
silver paint along the inner edges of the window
and along the outer edge of the foam; let dry.

**3** Punch five evenly spaced holes along the top
of the foam. Attach an eyelet (see page 6)
into each hole. Thread a jump ring (see page 13)
through each eyelet, then attach a ring onto each
eyelet ring.

**4** Glue the cardstock to the lower back of the
foam. Crop the photo to 1⅝"x3⅛" then
glue it to the cardstock centered inside the foam
window.

**5** Cut a 12" length of wire and thread it through
the top jump rings. Wrap each wire end
around a magnet until the magnets are 6" apart.
Cut two 4" lengths of wire and wrap one length
around each magnet. Use the wire cutters to cut the
shanks from the buttons. Attach a button to each
magnet with a Glue Dot™.

# Butterfly Brooch

rubber stamps:
  Zebra Butterfly
  Elsbet's Hatbox
chalk inks:
  Blue Shadow
  Pacific Horizon
  Lavender
    Flower
  Brushed Sage
pigment inks:
  gold
  gold ink refill
  gold embossing
    powder
beige craft foam:
  two 2½"
    squares
  one 1"x2"
    rectangle
1½"x2" white
  cardstock

1½" long jewelry
  pin
½" wide brass
  daisy button
2¾"x2¼"
  rectangle of
  burlap
embroidery floss
  metallic green
  metallic blue
¼" wide flat
  paintbrush
wire cutters
foam sponges
low temperature
  glue gun, glue
  sticks
embossing heat
  tool

**1** Sponge (see page 7) a combination of Pacific Horizon, lavender and green inks onto each of the craft foam pieces. Dip the paintbrush into the gold ink refill bottle and randomly brush it onto the foam pieces. Use another sponge to blend all the ink colors.

**2** Stamp *Elsbet's Hatbox* onto the foam squares and *Zebra Butterfly* onto the foam rectangle with Blue Shadow ink. Allow the foam to dry thoroughly. Cut out each stamped image shape.

**3** Wipe the burlap piece with the gold ink stamp pad, sprinkle gold embossing powder on top of the wet ink and heat set (see page 9).

**4** Use the wire cutters to cut off the shank from the back of the button. Glue the button centered on top of the foam butterfly. Cut a 6" length of each floss, fold them in half and glue the fold to the butterfly back. Fray the floss ends.

**5** Glue the butterfly to the top left corner of a *Elsbet's Hatbox* piece. Glue the piece angled on top of the remaining *Elbet's Hatbox* piece. Glue the foam pieces centered on the gold side of the burlap piece and let dry.

**6** Glue the cardstock piece centered on the burlap back. Glue the pin centered near the top of the cardstock piece.

## Stamping on Craft Foam:

The pliable surface of craft foam is perfect material for children learning to stamp. And it's as versatile as your child's imagination. They'll be thinking of new ways to use this inexpensive craft material in no time!

# Candles

Add a designer touch to candles with rubber stamping. Stamp directly onto the wax surface (after heating) or stamp on vellum or tissue and glue it to the candle side. As with all candles, use care when burning decorative candles and never leave them burning unattended.

# Calligraphy Candle Trio

Chinese Calligraphy (set of 3) rubber
    stamps
gold pigment ink
3 white votive candles
two saucers or cookie sheets
scrap paper
embossing heat tool

P*ractice stamping on an old candle until you feel comfortable with the process.*

**1** Cover your work area with scrap paper to protect the surface from melted wax.

**2** Apply gold ink to *Fortunate* from the *Chinese Calligraphy* set and set aside. Lay one of the candles on its side. Prop it in place with a saucer or cookie sheet on each side. (You can use other items that are low and resist heat to prevent the candle from rolling, such as wooden rulers or chop sticks.)

**3** Use the embossing heat tool on the wax for 5–10 seconds to to prepare the wax without melting it. When the wax turns cloudy, quickly stamp *Fortunate* into the warm wax, slightly rolling it along the cylindrical shape and allow it to set for 1–2 seconds. When the candle has cooled, carefully pull the stamp up and away from the candle and allow to dry. (Note: the imprint will retain some of the pigment ink, creating an antique effect.)

**4** Repeat steps 2–3 for *Joy* and *Friend* on the other two candles.

# Heirloom Candle

Filigree Corner rubber
  stamp
pigment inks:
  Chianti
  gold
embossing powders:
  gold
  clear
Paper Pizazz® ivory
  vellum

3"x2½" ivory pillar
  candle
double-sided adhesive
  paper
X-acto® knife, cutting
  surface
1" wide foam brush
liquid acrylic all-
  purpose sealer
embossing heat tool

**1** Seal the candle sides and let dry. Stamp *Filigree Corner* onto the vellum twice with gold ink. While the ink is still wet, sprinkle gold embossing powder on top and heat set (see page 9).

**2** Stamp *Filigree Corner* onto the vellum once with Chianti ink. While the ink is still wet, sprinkle clear embossing powder on top and heat set.

**3** Adhere each image onto the adhesive paper. Place each image on the cutting surface and use the knife to cut out each image, following the shape as closely as possible.

**4** Peel off the back of the adhesive paper from the Chianti stamped image and press it onto the candle as shown. Adhere a gold image on each side.

## Vellum embellishments:

The vellum embellishments on the candle are flammable. If you burn the candle, it is recommended you allow it only to burn above the vellum embellishments.

# Stamped 3-Wick Candle

Baroque Border rubber stamp
Painted Desert chalk ink
gold pigment ink
6" wide ivory 3-wick pillar candle
10mm glass tube beads:
  2 red
  2 amber
embroidery floss:
  metallic gold
  dark red
foam sponge
old towel
embossing heat tool

**1** Place the candle in the center of the towel. Ink *Baroque Border* with red ink. Use the embossing heat tool on a 2"x4" section along the bottom edge for 8-10 seconds to prepare the wax without melting it. When the wax turns cloudy, quickly stamp *Baroque Border* into the warm wax, slightly rolling it along the cylindrical shape and allow it to set for 1–2 seconds. Repeat the process for the next section and continue until the base of the candle is covered.

**2** Turn the candle upside down and repeat the stamping process to form a stamped border along the top edge.

**3** Sponge (see page 7) red ink along the top and bottom edge of the candle; let dry. Randomly sponge (see page 8) gold ink along the top and bottom edges, then carefully heat set, making sure not to melt the wax.

**4** Cut a 24" length of each color floss. Wrap the lengths around the center of the candle so they crisscross in the center and knot to secure. Thread an amber bead onto each red floss tail and knot to secure. Repeat with each red bead on the gold floss tails. Trim each tail to 1½"–2".

S tamp directly into sealing wax for a spectacular effect. Use sealing wax as the focal point of your project or add it as a finishing touch to seal an envelope or special note.

# Travel Wax Frame

rubber stamps:
  Far Off Posts (set of 4)
  Lettre
chalk inks:
  Spanish Sand
  Espresso
  Evergreen

pigment inks:
  copper
  black
sealing wax disks:
  2 gold
  2 silver
gold acrylic paint

7"x5" brown paper frame with
  an oval opening
metallic embroidery floss:
  silver
  gold
wax paper
foam sponge

craft stick
Glue Dots™
1/2" wide paintbrush
5"x3½" photo
embossing heat tool

**1** Remove the inserts from the frame. Stamp *Lettre* repeatedly around the frame with tan ink; heat set (see page 9). Randomly stamp (see page 8) each of the four images from *Far Off Posts* onto the frame with brown and green inks; heat set. Sponge (see page 7) the inner and outer frame edges with brown ink and heat set.

**2** Place one gold sealing wax disk on the wax paper. Ink one of the *Far Off Posts* stamps with black ink and set aside. Use the embossing heat tool to melt the wax to an irregular 1¼" circle. Let it cool for 5–10 seconds, then press the stamp into the

wax and allow it to sit for one minute. Lift the stamp carefully from the wax. Repeat the process for each of the sealing wax disks and stamps, using different stamps with copper ink for the remaining gold wax and alternating colors for the silver wax disks. Allow to cool completely.

**3** Lightly brush each wax piece with gold paint and let dry. Cut three 4" lengths of each floss, hold them together and attach them to the frame with a Glue Dot™. Add a wax piece as shown. Place a Glue Dot™ behind each remaining wax piece and attach to the remaining corners. Insert a photo into the frame.